The Jesus Book

Messages for the 21st Century

By Linda Dillon

Dedication

For Yeshua
And all who have the courage to walk the Jesus Path.

Table of Contents

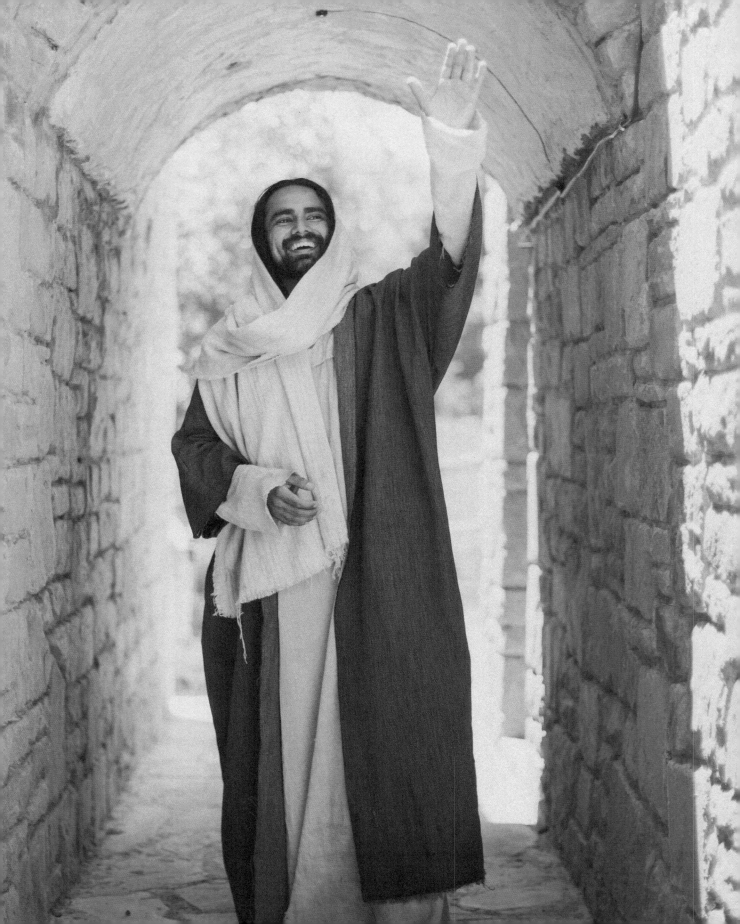

THANKS & GRATITUDE

Where do I begin with my acknowledgements and heartfelt thank-yous? The danger in creating acknowledgements is forgetting someone, or making them feel that somehow their contribution was underrated. That is simply not possible here. I have so much to be grateful for. The support I have received for many years has been phenomenal. This is the abbreviated version so if you don't see your name listed, please look up, and see it written in the heavens. Each of you has graced my journey in loving insightful ways.

I begin my acknowledgements with my soul family, with that circle of sweet Annas who have supported me every step of the way. This book would not have been happened so rapidly if it was not for the loving and practical support of the organization, collection and editing team who assisted me in the fulfillment of this promise to Jesus. Thank you from the bottom of my heart to Lorraine McGovern, Ellen Nairn, Deborah

9

Lifton, Traci Ortega, Marti Senterfit, Mary Valanzano, Elizabeth Farrington, Megann Thomas, Jeannette Reed, Yasmin Tirado, Dottie Chandler, Andrea Quagenti, Ruth Seymour, and Rose Rayne.

A special heartfelt thank you goes to the editing and review team, Marti Senterfit, Suzanne Dillon and Micki Mercurio. Together these angels have read every word of The Jesus Book and have poured out their hearts and souls to ensure it is the reflection of love. They have spent countless hours reviewing, editing, suggesting and improving the content, flow and final offering of this work.

My deepest thanks also goes to Jeri Burgdorf who has walked with me through this entire creation process. Jeri has tirelessly and lovingly worked with the entire volunteer team, edited, reviewed, hand-held the group, and so much more. Thank you, Jeri.

There has been a small legion of soul family who has and do support me in becoming who I am. There have been times when the encouragement and support has been emotional, spiritual and even financial. They have never let me give up and have continued to remind me that I am here on purpose, and that means service to the plan of the Mother/Father/One. I don't know if I would still be here without my family, especially my sisters, Suzanne and Debay, and my brother, Joe. The same is true of my soul sisters: Mare Valanzano, Roz Lett, Marianne Baer, Yasmin Tirado, Joanna

Brock, Jeri Burgdorf, Suzanne Wendelken, Marga Van Der Meijs, and Carol Bakunas. You have propped me up and reinforced me through the good and hard times. You remind me that this is all worth it—we are changing the world, one person at a time.

I also wish to acknowledge and embrace the love and support of my InLight Radio/Golden Age of Gaia family: Steve Beckow, Suzanne Maresca, Karen Wilson, Mike Heule, Paul Backes, and Ellen Nairn. The support and inspiration of this team has lifted me up, challenged me to grow, and taught me a deeper meaning of patience, fortitude and love.

The list of thanks could be endless for there are many of you that I love and who have been so generous with your energy and support. I want to say a special thank you to my Council of Love family who has traveled with me for so long—to Sedona, Michigan, New York, Florida, Colorado, California, and Arizona.

A huge thank you also goes to my husband, Isaac Cubillos, whose talent, patience, technical and design expertise has brought this book to production.

This book is truly a group effort; a mission of service. But, of course, the final responsibility for this book remains with me. And Jesus—not one word has been inserted without His agreement. So the errors are mine, the fulfillment is His.

My final thank you is to Jesus for trusting me with such an incredibly important undertaking. And a thank you to the entire Council of Love, our unseen friends of the highest order. Little did I know or even begin to comprehend the change in direction my life would take the day I first heard, "Welcome from the Council of Love." I am eternally grateful and blessed. Thank you for helping me remember who I am and why I came. I wouldn't change it for the world.

NOTE: Some of the terms in this book may be unfamiliar to you. For more information or to explore, please visit www.counciloflove.com.

INTRODUCTION

Can you imagine Jesus asking you to do something for him? What would you do if Jesus asked you to undertake a mission that was important to him?

That's what happened to me in March 2016 when Jesus came to me, and asked if I would publish all the messages He's brought forth through me for the past twenty-plus years. In the wee hours of the morning, Jesus spoke to me how His messages of love have never changed, and that it was time for all people of the planet to hear His words once again—His messages for the twenty-first century.

Our beloved master isn't speaking about a book for a select audience who reads channeled material. He is reminding everyone on Earth of all persuasions that the beginning, middle and end of this journey is about love.

Jesus wants us to remember that His messages are as applicable today as they were two-thousand years ago, perhaps even more so. There was an urgency to His request, a sense of right now, spread the word and remind everybody of the Good News. Remind everyone of the hope, joy and necessity of remembering that only love is real.

This request excited me beyond imagination, and it scared me silly. When I first began to channel it took me years to admit to myself, and then a couple of more years to admit publicly, that I was bringing forth Jesus. That declaration initially seemed blasphemous, egotistical and would place me far too clearly in the limelight.

Heck, it took me years to admit to speaking with Archangel Gabrielle! But Jesus? It's one thing to admit to channeling angels and guardians; it's a whole other thing to admit to channeling Jesus. But long ago I made a promise to Jesus not only to be true to the honor of being (one of) His channels but to do whatever it takes to bring to fruition His teachings and promise of love.

What our beloved Jesus was asking me to be is courageous; to have the courage of my convictions to step forward; to follow in His footsteps, and be willing to share the messages of love. No matter how challenging or nervous-making, how could I ever dream of turning away?

And, as He pointed out to me that night and so many other times as this book has unfolded, these messages are desperately needed again today, right now, and more than ever. We need to be reminded that we are the inheritors of this Earth; we are the fulfillment of the promise; we have been born to bring forth this experience of love— loving ourselves, and one another.

And so we began. The messages of Jesus have always touched my heart, stirred the knowing deep within. But what happened as we began this process of bringing together all the messages is that the flow, the strength, and the consistency of His love, His strength and His trust in each of us flooded forth.

While the overarching theme of this book is love, there are two repeating messages that emerge. The first is "Come walk with me." This invitation is our beloved master reaching out to us, again and again. Jesus is reminding us that we never walk alone. He is with us at all times—in the moments of deepest despair and greatest victory. He is our guide, our teacher, our mentor.

But more than that, Jesus reminds us that He is our brother and our dearest friend. He is with us, each of us, every step of the way. He asks us to walk with him, reminding us of our partnership in the fulfillment of the Divine Plan. He does not ask us to follow but to go forth with him. His strength is our strength. His trust is our trust. His knowing is our knowing. His creations can be our creation—the creation of a world where love is not only the watchword but the pattern of belief and behavior for all people. He reminds us because so many of us have forgotten.

The second theme is "My message does not change." While these words would seem self-evident, again it is His reminder. Whether it was in 33 A.D., or today, Jesus's message has never changed. His messages are those of hope, of bringing forth a world based on love, equality, and freedom for everybody.

His messages are reminding us of our divinity, of our ability to courageously step forward and be the light of God. To not hide our light under a bushel basket but to feel confident enough to admit our mistakes and go forward in the certainty not only that we forgive and are forgiven but that we have the wherewithal, the grace, to be that light of Christ.

Jesus is, and has been, known by many names: Jesus of Nazareth, Jesus Christ, Jesus Sananda, Jeshua, Yeshua, Savior, Lord, Master, Son of God and Prophet, to name a few. All these names refer to the same person, that same energy: our beloved teacher and brother who comes forth to remind us once again of who *we* are. He has adapted His words and message to the twenty-first century—and yet, His message does not change.

In these messages, Jesus clarifies many questions. He speaks to us about His life, His experiences and feelings, His marriage to Mary Magdalene, reincarnation, the time between His crucifixion and resurrection.

No subject has been out of bounds. No areas which have been previously debated but unanswered have been ignored.

Jesus is equipping us for our next steps; not shielding us in traditional ways but speaking to us as faithful brothers and sisters who have the courage to hear the truth and proceed with creating a planet of love. A planet not based on religious, social, cultural, or national beliefs but based on the holy truth of love for all life.

This is not the book I expected to be writing at this time. This is not based on my interpretations or experiences of the Jesus messages. The messages speak for themselves.

The love and energy of these words is beyond measure. It is a transmission of Jesus's love directly into your heart. Open your hearts and receive. Now is the time. Take from these pages the words that speak to your heart. Take the hope, courage, strength and love that our beloved master so generously and clearly offers us. Share them. Act on them. Anchor them in your heart.

So to return to my question: What would you do if Jesus asked you to undertake a mission for him? My beloved friends, Jesus is asking you—each of us and all of us—to step forward and walk with Him. He's asking, inviting and reminding us that we're here to live out His message and truth. I'm saying yes. Are you?

CHAPTER 1
WALK WITH ME

My beloved brothers and sisters, so often the Christian world refers to me as savior, while others refer to me as prophet. I wish to speak to you this day as friend. I want to speak to your heart in a way I haven't done in such a long time.

Come Walk with Me

I come this day as your brother and your friend to ask you once again to walk with me. I know it has been well over two-thousand years, but my request has not changed. I ask you to walk with me, and accompany me in the fulfilment of my Father and Mother's business. The job is enormous, but it is not only that. I do not wish to walk alone, much the same as you do not wish to walk alone.

You ask me to elaborate about what it means to walk with me—whether there will be a paycheck or what the rewards will be. It's true that there were many times when we worried about the bills and how we would feed the many mouths that would show up at our home: whether there would be money for cloth, whether there would be money to tithe, and even render our taxes.

You know that these things are all important in physical reality, that they are as important today as they were two-thousand years ago. I know what it is to worry about this. And I know what it is to be asked to

move about the world and speak in ways that are often disdained or at best misunderstood.

Nevertheless, I ask you to walk with me. If you choose not to do so, then who will?

The Mother has said that I will not incarnate, I will not take form again until war is over. There are many faces to war, but Archangel Michael's battle—Michael's war—is being won, heart by heart by heart.

Although I am not physically in form as yet, I prepare the way as once my cousin John once did. For some of you, it means leaving your nets untended—but not forever, leaving your computers off—but not forever—and for some of you, it means turning your computers on.

I ask you to help me share and spread the messages of love. It is the only good news worth reporting on Earth. You are love. I am love. We are love. And in this, we will love our neighbors. We will honor our neighbors. We will heal our neighbors. We will teach our neighbors, and we will show them the way, not through dogmatic rigors, but through gentleness, through play, through joy, through fun. And it is in this way that is so attractive, that millions upon millions upon millions will join us.

I am not asking you to become a priest or preacher; it is not yet time to go to the square and begin the preaching. What I am asking you to do is to walk with me, not as stranger but as friend, as disciple and brother, as sister, as co-creator.

Never did I intend to create monoliths and institutions that bound people in guilt. That is not the way of love. It does not matter whether it is called church or government. It is not the way of love, and it must be broken.

How this is broken is through gentleness and a pulling away from that understanding, leaving the illusion vacant. When there is no energy in the illusion it simply crumbles. That is the way it works. You do not need to spend hours, days and years trying to destroy it; simply walk away and it will crumble under its own weight. We will create new cities of light, new cities of love that are truly based in the unity and community—the truth of who we are.

You know the story of the Sermon on the Mount, the story of the loaves and fishes, the story of Cana. There was always enough. There was always enough to feed, to clothe, and to share a toast.

If the beginning of the day did not provide, then I would pray. I would pray and sometimes that which was needed would simply appear, and sometimes my friends the fishermen would bring the fish. It matters not, for both are miracles.

I am not the only one that is capable of miracles of creation. You will do all this and more in my name. Who do you think I was talking about?

I haven't changed. I want us to sit together, to break bread together, to share the stories of our hearts, our victories and our sorrows. I want to walk with you. That is my plea to you this day. Answer me with your heart, your invitations, and your actions.

My friends, I love you. Let me stand by you now, and let us go forward together.

Go in peace. Hosanna, hosanna, hosanna.

My Message Does Not Change

It is time, my sweet brethren, to leave the dusty road and come and sit by the water's edge. In silence and friendship, let's rediscover the stories of each other's heart.

My yearning is to help you dream, go forward, and receive. Not to strive, obtain, or accomplish, but to simply receive. You yearn that the dream may expand, for always the message of love has been far larger than a single planet or even a single galaxy. It is time, my friends, to expand your view.

Know that you are not a tiny, minute microcosm sitting in a huge universe, but that you are in the intersection of hope and creation. You are at the center of love, and you have this to send to many, but first and foremost to your sweet self. My message does not change. Worth is not measured by financial statements, institutions or another human being. It exists as fact within the heart and mind of God.

He did not send me to speak of love to a race of slaves. I am here to destroy the illusion that you are less than whole. It is time to celebrate, to drink the wine of life and feasting, to close the circle and to reunite. It is time for us to regather, for there is much to be done.

I have beckoned you to go forward with me so we may show the way for all.

Jesus's Dream

I join you in love and wholeness, support and dreaming. Allow me to take your hand, for I am part of your sacred circle and always have been. You are in a time of massive, rapid change and that is the best news I can bring to you. It is what we have all awaited and prayed, worked, participated, and observed. These are part of creation. I know we have spoken in several different ways, but I wish to speak to you and to your hearts intimately.

My friends, we have had many conversations about creation and co-creation. Certainly the co-creation of Nova Earth, Nova Being, Nova Society, and Nova Reality is well underway. But I am asking you to take more time to dream—not just to visualize—but to allow your heart and mind and your very soul essence to soar and to begin to dream the new reality.

You do not arrive in the fifth, sixth or seventh dimensions with it all pre-con-

structed. This is not a prefab job. While there are many elements in place, there are also elements that will absolutely be missing as you leave behind the old paradigms of the third dimension. And that is good news to all of us and certainly to all of you. Out of the dreaming comes what you are choosing to create and co-create, and the unity of your being, and the unity of this circle, of what you wish to bring forward in terms of environments, and concretely in terms of buildings, situations, institutions, and ways of doing things.

My beloved wife and I used to spend a great deal of time together dreaming. And yes, each of us was fully aware of the very likely unfoldment of our life and our family's life together during my incarnation as Jeshua, and hers as Mary Magdalene. But that did not stop us from dreaming. The reason I bring this up, my dear hearts, is that she and I dreamed this time: This time when peace would be restored, where love would reign on earth; where freedom would be the air that all beings breathed; where sweetness would be the way, and gentleness would be the watchword of how people would treat each other and how communities would live. The foundation was laid so long ago, long before my incarnation.

The Divine Plan of our Mother is not only infinite, it is eternal, but this portion of it, this fulfillment of it, and yes, this vision of it was something that Mary and I spent time thinking, dreaming, and talking about. It made it all worthwhile. I've been human as is she, and we know in human terms that time sometimes stretches, and you say, "When will this take place? When will we see the tangible shift?" My beloved friends, you are the tangible shift. Look in the mirror and see how you perceive yourself and your world around you. You are fully moving into your role as Creator Race and that is why I am asking you to join my beloved and me in the dreaming, because frankly my friends, most of you are dreaming too small.

I don't wish to minimize your burdens. For some of you it is health challenges, for others it is money and finance. I remember Caesar's coinage along with unjust taxation and unjust imprisonment. There are many kinds of imprisonment, you know. For some of you it is loneliness as you yearn for your spiritual family and your unique partner. I do not minimize that because I know of the heaviness of your heart.

But if I could ask you to just set these burdens slightly aside as if you are constructing something out of building blocks or Legos on a dining room table. Take those worries and put them off in a corner to your right-hand side where we can take care of them and then leave the rest of the table clear for your dreaming and building. And in that building and construction of the reality that you see and foresee and are participating in creating; all of those old issues which are simply telltale signs of the third dimension will be addressed.

As you dream, dream of community so that you are holding hands with those you love. Gather around that dining room table holding hands as you give blessings for the food that you have all co-created, and had a great deal of fun doing so. Share the laughter and sweetness so that vision and closeness is repeated all up and down the streets of every community all over your planet. See that there is food on every table and fresh water to drink, and if it is a wedding, I will provide the wine.

I am asking you to expand. Expand your vision and begin to truly build, because all is underway. It is not some distant date. You are already shifted. Gaia is firmly entrenched in the fifth through the seventh dimension of Christ consciousness. Your feet are upon her, therefore it is only the idea and belief system of the old third dimension that remains.

You are being freed up and I want you to go for this with the ease, grace and crystal clear clarity that you already have. And if you are not clear, if you are not sure, then come to the 13th Octave and rest there. We are all willing to help you because we are your family, as clearly as you are each other's family. We love you and there is nothing we would not do to assist you as you are assisting us, as each of you are fulfilling Mary's and my dream...the Mother's dream.

Let us go forward together in this creation and co-creation. Let there be no such thing as even a hint of a breeze that says imitation. Dream your world because it is yours and mine; it is Terra Nova. Then I can return, and I look forward to walking with you.

Welcome to the Twenty-First Century

This millennium of the twenty-first century belongs to love. I claim it as my own, and I do so in the name of my Mother and Father, and all throughout the universe.

You are not alone. It is time for this human race to remember this. You are our messengers. We have chosen you as our partners, and you have chosen us. I ask each of you to place yourselves beyond expectations and simply receive.

This does not mean there aren't many, many matters of a physical nature to be attended to each and every single day. When I lived with family, I learned my father's trade. But I did not work very hard. I had my spiritual work to do, and this was understood. I did not wake up, even as I traveled from town to town, wondering if I would have a meal that day. I was beyond expectations; I knew as a human being that I would be provided for.

This is what I ask of you: to let go of your expectations and fear, to let go of believing you will be in need. You are loved wholly and completely, more fully than you love yourself.

My job now and forever is to remove your doubt. I look at you and feel only love and acceptance. Let me be your mirror. Let me reflect this back to you. Look in this mirror and see not only my face but yours.

The anchoring of love upon Earth and the ripple effect throughout the planet is not done. It is not complete until there is an honoring of your own self. Allow this time of miracles, this millennium, to proceed with thanksgiving to you, and within the hearts of everyone upon the Earth. You are entering a new time and a new realm of existence.

Many of you say that finances are a recurring theme since the time of Abraham. This will be a time of prosperity throughout your land. It will be a time of prosperity that has never been known upon your Earth.

You are entering the time of creation, and that is what is leading to this prosperity. You are being gifted new technology, new thoughts, and new ways of understanding. It is expansion in every form. It's not just in spiritual form but right down to your toes, your feet, the very soil of Mother Earth, and the heart of the planet.

Be intelligent and follow your heart. Prudence, fortitude, and gratitude are the virtues that have been gifted to you through the heart of God. Practice them. Practice partnership in every form, but first with yourself.

Understand that this does not mean a continuation of business as usual. It means an absolute change—a shift in everything you do in the ways of relating, not simply in personal relationships. Family is ultimately the most important, but so is business. You cannot be kind and charitable within the walls of your home and go out and slit the throat of your competitor.

You cannot allow this to occur on your planet. It is not a matter of saying, "This is not my business." It is. It does not mean being confrontational. It means using the gifts at your disposal. You have been given many tools to call upon. Use them. Change yourself, use your energy, and change the world.

How do I define energy? I define it as love. I do not mean romantic love, although that is another gift. I define it as a feeling. It is the knowing and the behavior within you that communicates to **all, that you are of the vibration of One. How do you show it? You show it in your countenance. You show it in your eyes, your smile, your gentle touch and embrace. You show it in your silence which is often the best gift you can give another; to keep quiet.**

Do not try to figure out what you need or what you need to do; instead, figure out what your partners need. Take care of that first, and the rest will follow.

Opportunity for the Twenty-First Century

I wish to speak about the energy of this time. Time is opening up for you over the course of the next several years. This is a time of opportunity: a time of growth, expansion, acceptance and allowance of who you are. It is in the incorporation of the energies surrounding you. It is in the conscious, physical action choices—the choices of your heart, the decisions of your mind. For good what is opportunity without choices, decision, and action? It would be meaningless.

Opportunity has many faces, and it needs to be examined and embraced with unique discernment—outside the realm of judgment. Very often the human experience of judgment is completely erroneous. Think of my beginnings, dear one, which were not myth but actuality.

My beloved mother, the queen of heaven, had to labor on a donkey. I was born in a barn, swaddled in rags in a cradle of hay. We did not have any luxury other than the little bit that was given to us by the Magi, and fresh water. The people in your society would not say that this was great opportunity; they would say, "Oh no, he had a very rough start."

My beloved friends, the opportunity I was given to be born, to enter and be surrounded in this way was miraculous, for I was swaddled in my mother's womb and felt

"You are surrounded at this time, as you never have been before, not only with the energy of our Mother, but with the energy of many, including myself."

Her essence. I was protected and watched over by my beloved father, Jophiel. Kings, shepherds and angels gathered to welcome me, to celebrate with me, to celebrate my choice, my decision to incarnate and to walk the world, not only in service—but in love.

Opportunities grew as I grew; I was constantly in that energy field, penetrated by my mother and father and many who loved and cherished me.

This is what made me strong, secure and clear. This is what made me able to go forward in my choices, even when they went against the grain of my parents. Never did that support or love vary. This was my unique opportunity.

Why do I bring this up? Because, my beloved friends, you are being given exactly the same opportunity at this time. The Mother isn't simply showering from above. She is penetrating you in your household and your daily activities. She is standing next to you, behind you. Because of its potency, Her energy is penetrating directly through you whether you acknowledge it, know it, accept it or not. There were many times when I thought I was alone, when I thought I had solitude. I would sneak off, and still my mother's energy would penetrate me. She would know exactly what I was up to, as did my father.

You are surrounded at this time, as you never have been before, not only with the energy of our Mother, but with the energy of many, including myself. This is a unique opportunity. It is not just expansion, not just a change in frequency. It is a human opportunity.

It is an opportunity for you not only to choose, but to change and go forward in ways reflective of the truth of your dreams, of your heart, and who you wish to be. You are supported as never before.

This is a magnificent opportunity. It is one I was given, and now it has been given to all of you. It is not a matter of accepting or not accepting. It is in your very household. What will you do with it?

We pose the question to you, what do you choose, individually and collectively, to create this year, this lifetime? We ask so we may be involved in this creation—to assist you. If you never answer the question, then you aren't clear enough with yourself nor with us, nor the universe.

We are prepared to help you. It is not done for you; it is done with you in co-creation, in partnership. We do not assume to take care of you as a helpless infant, because you are not. Oh yes, you will have moments when you will feel that you are. Simply clear, let go and acknowledge your own strengths to stand with us in reverence—as we stand with you in reverence.

This is not about equality; this is about honoring what each being brings forth. It is a tapestry and you are an essential thread. Changes in the creation of Nova Earth are created from the choices of your heart:

whether it is to heal the rivers and waters, to recycle, to start a new career or start new relationships.

It is about a new relationship of self with self. It is about a deeper understanding of the opportunity to be alive; the opportunity to live in joy and in the expression of love.

Always it comes back to love; this will never change. You know that you are loved, but do you love and cherish yourself enough to trust and accept this opportunity?

I am with you. Many choose to call me Savior. I choose to call you brother and sister, family of my heart, of my very soul. When you wish advice, encouragement or a helping hand, turn to me and I will be there. I will not do for you, but I will show you what to do.

Go with my infinite love, my admiration. I give you my heart of joy and share with you opportunity. Go in peace.

CHAPTER 2
LOVE

My entire life upon the planet, my purpose for coming, my entire essence, my soul contract, as man and as son of God, is about the nature of love.

When I walked the Earth I had very simple messages, and they were about love: To love yourself and to love one another, as you love yourself. That is always the first step—that deep spiritual, emotional, mental, physical respect for self; that honoring, cherishing, affection, concern, kindness, consideration, compassion for your sacred self.

What is Love?

Love is a state of being. For a long time now, I have asked you to join with me in the seventh dimension, for this is the dimension of love. It seems that no matter how often I say this, very often it falls on deaf ears simply because you have not been ready to hear it. But I am saying it again.

Join with me through the 13th Octave into the seventh dimension. It is a state of being beyond physicality, and yet it can be anchored in physicality. It can be experienced in your third dimension as you know it, and in fact, it is so much fun!

I also came to Earth to have that experience of love in physical form just like each of you; to bring that energy of love and have it embodied in a physical vessel.

Many of you wish to die to know nirvana, bliss, wholeness. And yet to know love in form is wholeness. It is completion. It is in that state of wholeness that I wish you to live.

Love is a state of being in ultimate connection to One, to All. It is a state of being in joy. Many of you have great difficulties finding your joy these days. Go to the love; it will bring you to the joy. It is a state of being in union.

The keys to heaven are love, trust and forgiveness, unity, connectedness and balance. These are simply different points of the same currency, which is love; it is one thing.

Love is also action, not only on your physical plane or in different dimensions and realities. When we create, when Mother/Father/One births a new universe or a new reality, it is done from the place of love. It is the action of that union, the connectedness, which explodes into creation.

Love has many other examples of action: it is kindness to each other; it is consideration; it is being honest and truthful and standing in integrity; it is being compassionate and not even knowing the meaning of being judgmental. When you are in this state of being—of connection and love—you cannot be anything but kind, considerate, open, available, and a magnificent healer, teacher and role model.

Love is action, but it is also the silence of your being. It is being in the stillpoint; it

30

is being in the void of nothingness and still being ultimately and completely connected in One. I don't mean that as being out of form, but rather in your form.

Finally, love is expression. It is an experience that has no comparable experience; there is nothing on Earth or beyond that is greater than the experience of love. That is why I wanted to come to Earth; not only to teach about the continuation of existence and the ability to move in and out of form, but to also have the experience of love within myself, and from that to have the exchange with my family, my mother and father, my brothers and sisters, my beloved wife and children, my apostles, my disciples and my friends.

I came to learn to hold love even for those who did not return my love, and that was a lesson. I did not need to go into judgment or approve of their lives or their actions. I had no wish to pick up stones. I came to know that to give someone love, even when they despise you, is a gift to your own heart. The love is returned, perhaps not by that individual, but by the universe and by other human beings. Love is never wasted. The more you give, the more it grows, and the more you receive.

Love is being happy. It is being in that state of thanksgiving and gratitude, even when you think you are in your darkest hour. So often I hear your heart pleas to me, to Mother and Father, "I do not feel love; all I feel is alone and abandoned." For those of you, who sit in that darkness of your soul just let me in. I will come gently and illuminate your heart once again. I will anchor my consciousness within you, that you will know and be love once again, because that is the purpose.

There are many different soul and human contracts, many different pathways, but the entire purpose of being in form, of being alive, is to know and to be love. When you do that, you are doing everything else. You are fulfilling every expectation, mission, purpose and contract; you are doing it all.

I invite you to know love, to be love, without exception. It is the beginning and it is the end. It is the Alpha and the Omega. All the lessons, all the tools, all the messages that we have ever shared, regardless of culture or time—they are all about love.

It is about being in that state of wholeness and allowing. There are no shields when love is present. That is what I am going to teach you: how to live without these shields, how to live in connectedness and unity. It is our next step together. You are ready and I am excited.

Hold tight to each other, my friends. Pass this love from one heart to the next and receive it with gladness. It is the manna of your soul; it is the manna of your physical body, it is what makes you who you are.

Sweet angels, you are magnificent. You are my beloved ones. I love you.

"You seek love, you attract love and repulse that which is not love."

Give Me Your Shields

You may call me Jesus, or simply brother. I will not shield myself, because where there is love it will always win, always penetrate, always be the gift.

Yahweh has said, "Only those who are of love shall gather in this home." That is why you are here—to be the love. It entails courage, trust, and belief in us and in yourselves. Together, we are a unified field surrounded by magnificent angels gathered to witness the beauty of human beings choosing divinity, choosing love.

When you erect your shields, either through your personality, spiritual or emotional fields, you are saying, "I wish to be isolated." Let's be realistic – you can't be! It doesn't work; it never has and it never will. That does not mean that the uniqueness of your precious being is not noted and loved— it is. But it can only be fully acknowledged and contributed to when you are available. You have an expression in your generation, "They are not emotionally available," meaning they are shielded. Being shielded in this manner never reinforces love.

I ask of you to be united with me, not only in the 13th Octave, but always and everywhere. Wherever you are, I wish to be with you. Wherever I am, I am inviting you along—and that, my friends, is an adventure! So what do you say? Let us begin, for it is a new day.

The Power of Love

My brothers and sisters, I am not asking you to spend your time remembering the past. To draw upon it, most certainly, as you draw upon the future—the future that you create in this very moment. But where love lives is in the now. It is in this precious moment as you breathe the fuel of the universe, and that has not changed since I walked the Earth so long ago.

Like you, I came with a mission from the Mother and Father to create a new community based in love. The directive I received from my parents was simple: Go forward and help them remember the love, to love themselves and to love each other. Nothing more, nothing less, and this is what I tried to do.

I have heard your cries in the night when you have said, "Jesus, I don't think I'm getting through to these people; I don't think I'm making a difference. I don't think I'm moving forward fast enough; I don't think I'm good enough."

I feel the ache in your heart, and I hope you receive my comfort. I hope you hear my words and laughter because it's like listening to myself. How many times I would turn to my beloved wife and my parents and say, "I don't think I'm getting through to them," and we would laugh and we would rest; we would restore, and we would start again.

That is all there is: to love. It is the faithfulness, it is loyalty, it is stamina, it is fortitude. It is the ability to know beyond doubt, beyond fear who you really are—and you, my friends, are mighty and you are gentle. Love does not push. It may sound assertive in trying to persuade, but it doesn't push. It is convincing because of the gentleness; because of the solid strength of the oak tree.

I have spoken to you about my honor for my father in physical life, Joseph, and what he taught me in terms of being a man. I compare him to that oak; to that strength and solidity. That is also the quality of the male, the Divine Masculine that you bring forward. It is to stand strong against the winds, to protect everybody that lives underneath you and in you. It is the quiet teaching and holding of space. It is warming the people and families at the end of your life. It is providing shelter.

These are wonderful qualities to bring forward. Each one of you has a blessed uniqueness that you have chosen, that you have created with the Mother/Father/One/Source. Throughout all universes, throughout all realities, all dimensions, wherever you would search, you are unique. The gifts, the beauty, the love you carry—its expression—can only come from you in your unique way. Do not ever doubt it.

At times, you have touched the heart of another and thought, I did not get through. Then they go away and think about it and are transformed. You do not see all the results of your work, and you do not need

to. Your role is simply to be the vessel of transmission.

When you take away all that feeling of burden and responsibility for outcome, you lighten up. When you are in the fullness of who you are, when you are the embodiment of that, the outcome will be the love and the peace. So detach from worrying.

Brothers and sisters of my heart, my soul and my family, hold tight in this community. Be the unity of One. Be the unity of yourself. Anchor yourself firmly so that you are unshakeable, because you will be challenged. When you have the slightest shadow of doubt, simply turn to me. I am right there with you.

I do not think you hear often enough how well you are doing, the miracles that you perform every day. We are grateful to you. Our partnership is strong, our vision is clear. Our purpose is community, our purpose is joy. Our purpose is love.

Your Divine Pattern

My message does not change. Love is the essence of the universe: All that is, all that ever has been, and all that ever will be. And yet, what is this elusive quality, this element that we call love?

The patterning of the universe is aligned with the essence of the Divine Mother. I wish to discuss this with the entirety of your being—heart to heart, head to head, and body to body—for you to more deeply comprehend and embrace what this patterning means.

What is love? It is the very essence, the fabric, the subatomic particles, the nano particles of the Mother/Father/One. It is the elemental material from which all is created.

You may have thought of yourselves as carrying the spark of the divine light and essence within you. That's true, but it's also incomplete.

Often you have felt that there is a need to activate, attune, work, and struggle to ignite this spark of divinity within you in order to become the magnificence and true expression of who you are. That is an incomplete understanding.

Every fiber of your being, every unique hair upon your body, every cell of your skin, every element of your blood, organs and bones is patterned after, and a reflection of, the Mother/Father/One. It is who you are—not as a single spark, but as a totality.

It is not something that you choose; it is simply the reality of which you are constructed. It is not merely your foundation and not merely your heart, but every portion of you. That is why I say that we are talking about all of your bodies, all of your elements—your conscious, subconscious, and superconscious, your egocentric self, to your universal self. It is all comprised of love.

Amazing, isn't it? The real challenge is that in human form, in this physical arena which you are occupying at this time (and that has been occupied for thousands and thousands of years), it is difficult for you to know and comprehend what is not seen or tangible to your senses.

In the human realm, you know love through experience and expression. It is through the experience and expression of the elusive energy of love that you truly come to know, anchor, accept and be love. You work within the Mother's framework and Her creation of time. Think of time as brackets with infinity on one end and eternity on the other end. As a human in form, you would feel that you are free floating in space if you were not within these brackets that we call time.

Previously, and still to some extent, you see time as linear, as sequential. That is why you have such experiences of aging, of shifting within your own sacred self—as relationships, world unfoldment and growth, patterning and repatterning. This is so you can have this experience and this expression of love within a form.

Is that the totality of love? Of course not, but within the realm of humans, at this moment, that is how it is brought forth. These brackets of infinity and eternity are a construct; they are an illusion put in place by the Mother so you can operate and know what love looks, feels and is experienced as. Otherwise, it would be amorphous; it would feel as if you are chasing the proverbial pot of gold at the end of the rainbow that never ends and that you can never find. That is neither the Plan nor the desire of the Mother. The entire purpose of your being, in the collective sense, is for you to know and have this experience of love in physicality.

It is critical during this time of extraordinary change for you to comprehend, accept, receive, and anchor that you are nothing more and nothing less than love, the totality of the Mother's love. When you fully embrace this, there really isn't any room for distraction. Distraction is simply you flexing your psychic muscles as human beings. It is flexing your muscles and saying, "I have free will, I have free choice, and in this moment I choose to put my energies elsewhere." The distractions can be active or passive indifference, or even the embrace and dancing with the darkest dramas that exist upon your planet. It doesn't matter; it is simply distraction. When you are offered, begged and pleaded with to accept all there is, then why—in heaven or on Earth, above or below—would you even consider, let alone engage in distraction?

I have walked the planet and know the allure of distraction; I know the sexiness of flexing your muscles, the attractiveness of saying, "I simply need time out; I need to be distracted for the moment." That is a choice, but one that diminishes you. It is a choice of denial of your divine pattern, of

the truth and the essence of who you are. It is a statement of the soul saying, "I don't love and care about myself enough to pay attention or to be vigilant."

When I say to pay attention or to be vigilant, I am not asking you in any way, shape or form to be constantly on high alert; that is exhausting. I am simply asking, suggesting, guiding, that when you are observing and participating in this arena—in this interdimensional reality currently available to you upon Gaia—there are many distractions: family, self, politics, money, society.

There are times when you need to be fully participating in all of those realms. I am not talking about becoming a hermit or a recluse; I am not talking about shunning humanity and the collective. When you bring to your interactions the fullness, the innate understanding and embrace of who you are, then those interactions—those connections within that unified grid—shift enormously.

So, my beloved friends and family do not be distracted. Bring all your actions, within and without, to the full attention, knowing and presence of your mighty self—because you are the Mother's agents of change.

This is a time of extraordinary change, wherein ninety-nine-point-nine percent of the collective of humanity is in the process of anchoring into the physical realm, the reality of love. That is what ascension is; it is the rebirth of love as the modus operandi for Gaians. It is making each choice in alignment with your pattern and the Mother's pattern (they are one and the same) and making the consistent choices of love. The only way you experience this love is through its experience and its expression.

When I spoke to you thousands of years ago, I begged you to love your neighbor as yourself. There was no division and no separation in that statement—in the plea that I made to you then, and that I make to you again today. There is the love within and the love without according to Universal Law, of how things work upon your planet and everywhere else.

My message does not change. You are changing because you are more fully able to truly hear, integrate, anchor, and translate into action and form what I am saying. The core of that statement is to love yourself; that is the primary starting point of experiencing love.

You may say, "I love God, Source, Mother/Father/One"—but how do you know God? You know God because you know yourself; you know the pattern of who you are. You may not cognitively, emotionally, mentally fully comprehend what I am saying, but you know it because your soul, your higher self, your heart knows it; you know that you are love.

Look to the Universal Law of Attraction and Repulsion: you seek love, you attract love and repulse that which is not love. It begins with the love of this beautiful, remarkable, holy sacred self: not just your spirit, but your toes, fingers, hair, face and tummy. It starts with knowing and loving how you behave, what you say and do; from there you can love your neighbor, which is every single person upon the planet.

Love is cyclical; it is the flow of the infinity. As you love others, as you embrace the collective, that love grows. As you share love it grows and as it grows and expands you open and receive in the infinite flow and wonder of the infinity. This is the balance of the give and take, the above and below—and in that you know the love of Source, of Mother/Father/One. This is the pattern of the universe.

It is mind-boggling, is it not, to think of yourself as an equal point, an equal player on that ebb and flow of the infinite? Yet, you are equal with the mighty ones, with the ascended ones, with All and with every other being—including those who pursue distraction vigorously.

At times, can this feel like a heavy load? Yes, it can and I know whereof I speak. But, my beloveds, it is also the greatest joy you will ever experience; it is the greatest expression of you that can ever come forth while in form.

Each of you has been entrusted as an equal: you, with your unique individual soul design. Your unique talents are essential to this shift in form, and consciousness, upon this planet. It is overwhelming—in the sense of awe and supreme wonder at the expression of the Mother's Divine Plan that is in immediate unfoldment.

You are up to the tasks at hand. My desire is that you will choose and allow your sacred sweet self to experience, receive and express—up close and personal—my love for each of you.

I am with you. If you accept this gift. It allows me to continue my mission and purpose to serve you, and to serve the Mother.

Love: The Practical Choice

Often you are seeking the secrets of divinity; the understanding of Universal Law, how things work throughout the multiverse, how you will ascend and what that process will be like.

Let me break it down to the nuts and bolts. In any reality; above, below or anywhere in between—the only state of being in which you can maintain yourself is by choosing love. It is that straightforward.

You want to understand the mysteries of the universe. When you practice love—when you choose and incorporate love into your very being, the mysteries and complexities you mistakenly assign to the universe, disappear.

When you do not choose love, you make your life more difficult than it needs to be. In your old third dimensional reality, so much effort went into the maintaining of false grids and illusions. What did this accomplish? It accomplished false insti-

tutions, false understandings about how relationships work or don't work, false understandings about what you are capable of. The most destructive, from my perspective, is the belief that you would have to earn love. That is not so.

When you choose to simply be who you are, you are simplifying your life because you are choosing love. You are eliminating the drama, chaos, uncertainty and everything that is not of wholeness.

Uncertainty is a theme right now the human collective is dealing with—as release and final clearing of lack of love. Uncertainty means, "I am not positive about the outcome; therefore, I am stuck. I am stuck in worry, fear and anxiety. Rather than living in the present, I am fearful of moving backwards or forwards because I am not sure; I am not certain."

When you simply be love—in your breath, your heart, your thoughts, your actions—then uncertainty simply disappears; there is no place for it.

The bigger understanding of ascension (expansion into heart consciousness) is the fact that it too is of love. It is a mirror of how you are, who you are, and how you operate within the multiverse; being in this understanding allows you to let go of everything that has ever plagued you.

It is true there is a human inclination to want to know. I understand and have lived that. But, you will still only know a portion of the outcome. I can describe what lies ahead for hours and hours, days and centuries—but the ingredient that matters in that formulation of what lies ahead, is you. If you are spending your time and energy in uncertainty, insecurity, fear and worry, then that is what you are creating. And that is not practical.

Knowing that you exist infinitely and eternally, I also want you to focus on this life that you have created and chosen with us, with your guides, with those you journey with—because this is the moment that you are in; that is what we mean when we are talking about the eternal now. It is not a beginning and an ending; it is all right now. In your framework and understanding, all you have is this very moment.

In this moment, do you choose love or do you choose worry? Do you choose hatred or control; greed or distrust? There really isn't any choice when I put it that way, is there? My Magdalena and I had a clear understanding of what lay ahead. We could have decided not to come together, not to share our hearts, our love. We could have chosen not to create a family, so that we could simply worry about what lay ahead. We could have worried and complained about persecution, unfairness and injustice.

Then I would have defeated my very purpose in coming, because I would not have chosen love.

When I walked with my apostles, disciples, my family, I could have said, "I know the time will come when some of you will deny or betray me, so I am not going to break bread with you now. I am not going to share a cup of wine with you now because, although you say you are my friend, I know I am going to be heartily disappointed later."

I was never disappointed, because I knew the love was always there. This is the thing I wish to address, because you often skirt it. You declare that there are times when people can disappoint you; that is simply not true.

You can choose to be disheartened or disappointed; you can choose to feel betrayed. But what does that do? It robs you of your love in your moment.

Each and every breath, every moment of your existence make the practical, easy choice: Choose love. It is easy; it is far more difficult to stir up wrath or fear, than to simply stay in your heart, in the knowing that in your core you are love.

Love is who you are. The more you accept and know that, the more it comes to you, and the more you generate. You send it out to the planet, and then you all proceed together; it is as simple as that.

Loving in this way is not what you are used to. It is what we have termed the "new normal," and it is the original design. You are designed to understand this. Yes, there are times when situations develop to help you understand the importance of the mirrors in your life which you think of as good, bad, evil, dark, light or even indifferent.

Consider for a minute the devastation that leads an individual, or groups of individuals, to a place where they do harm. It doesn't matter whether it is dropping a nuclear bomb, polluting the air, hurting a child, raping, the list goes on. For someone, anyone, to be that lost is tragic.

How can such tragedy be healed? Only by love. Love is the essence and the core, the building blocks, the subatomic particles, of the entire universe. It is the essence of All. Unless there is love generated, transmitted into that situation or person, there cannot be a shift to heart centered actions and knowing.

Often, when those who veer, shall we say, "into the darkness," they have a moment where they "see the light" and return to the light. They think of it as divine intervention. But what is divine intervention, except that miniscule opening within that person's heart to receiving love?

Very often it is because someone on Earth has sent the love and healing. You did not come to be judge and jury. There can be no judgment ever in love, because if you are in judgment you are not in love. You are robbing yourself.

There is a difference between judging and being discerning, which indicates that you are in the place of being the observer. In being the observer, you see the tragedy and you can send the love. There is much

emphasis and discussion about forgiveness: "Oh, I must forgive this person, or that person, or this situation; I must forgive myself." But if you are in love, this is already done. It's already taken care of.

Love literally moves you to the higher plane, and it is the higher plane that I have spoken of for millions and millions of years. It is where I invite you to join me. Is it important that you love your enemy as yourself? Yes; my message does not change.

It is easy to love someone who loves you back, who mirrors all the divine qualities you cherish. What you don't know, and what I invite you to learn with me right now, is that it is also easy to love all beings equally. This may come as an aha moment when you decide, "I love myself, warts and all." It is not fireworks or the Fourth of July; it is more subtle. It is the quiet awakening from a very, very deep sleep, a deep sleep of illusion.

Many lightworkers cry, "I have not ascended; I have not had the grand shift in consciousness that I have been wanting and praying for; awaiting eagerly." We share your eagerness in this, you know. That shift to holding love and light is the most important aspect of this shift.

If you are still in the place of judgment and justification of your behavior and your lower emotions, begin to practice more love. As you wake up, think to yourself, "I had a very good sleep and I feel better today—I feel as if I could love the world." Then do it. That is not to say there are no blips. When you find yourself in one of those little detours, be gentle and laugh; say to me, "Oh, Jesus, there I go again," and come back.

Ranting and being angry takes you away from who you are. You can shake your head and say, "I do not know the outcome, I do not know what lies ahead—but I do know that I am loved." In that is the full knowing that you are attended to by the wholeness of your sweet self, the company of Heaven, the mighty archangels, the Mother/Father/One, your human brothers and sisters, and by me.

There are times when you find it difficult to send love to those you disdain. You are finding those challenges because you are in judgment. There also can be memories or a soul resistance. Allowing the Mother's love to flow through you washes this away. You do not revert back to the fault, blame, guilt, shame. Instead, stay in the stillness until Her love penetrates you, and brings you to that place of acceptance of your wholeness yet again, so that you can continue on. It is so peaceful, so pleasurable, so sweet that you will never want to go back.

There will be times when you feel rejected or abandoned by those you believe have loved you. You rant and rave, from a place of ego, about these hurts. When this occurs, and it will, let the tears come. They are the tears of your soul and your heart yearning for love. Your ego, of course, would like you to stop the tears and gain control.

But that does not serve you. What you are crying for is love. So, let my love fill you until it becomes so apparent that you think, "If I am that loved by Jesus, then perhaps I can love myself as well."

That knowing will overflow into your heart, into your being and personality— allow it to do so. When you are back in a place of loving and cherishing yourself, then love will come to you in friendship, family and yes, in a beloved form.

This is not some magic formula. I know what it is to feel that your heart is broken. I ask of you, in this moment, to agree and to allow it to mend. Let me help you.

Love makes your life fuller. I am not suggesting that you spend twenty four hours a day in meditation allowing yourself to be filled with love. Although there are times, sweet angels, when that is necessary because you are that depleted.

I am talking about the practical choices. As you go into the kitchen, ask yourself, "What refreshes me like love? Is it water, juice, tea, caffeine? What tastes like love?" Look in your refrigerator or your cupboard and think, "How do I feed myself love?"

You walk outside, whether in a metropolis or an isolated area, and you breathe the air, the sweet breath of Gaia, which is love. You see the downtrodden, and perhaps you feel that you are amongst the downtrodden, so you send love to yourself and to them.

When you are in a place of uncertainty,

insecurity, of not knowing what lies ahead, pull yourself back, right into the moment. Not tomorrow, not an hour from now, and certainly not yesterday. In the moment, feel my love—and be the love that you are. That is all that is ever required; it is the key to everything.

That is why I say, especially in this time, love is the practical choice. If you wish to make your life easier, more joyous, more fulfilled, more abundant, richer in every sense of the word—choose love.

When you feel torn between what you judge as responsibility and what your heart desires, it can create an inner conflict. How do you choose between what you feel guided to do, and the love and demands of family? I am sorry; there is no choice. There is only love.

But it is strong bedrock love. Understand what I say to you: There were times, even as a young man, that my mother—and sometimes my Magdalena - would ask if I had to go out and make a public statement. "You know, you're aggravating the Pharisees; you know they're watching you; couldn't you just stay home?"

It was up to me—not my mother, not my wife, not even my beloved children. It was up to me to make that choice. No one could make it for me; no one can make it for you.

Let me speak of the duality that you are leaving behind. In duality/polarity, you feel trapped in the belief system of "either/or."

It also relates to the belief system: "I only have limited energy; I only have limited time; I only have limited capacity in which to apply myself." My beloved friend, that's not true.

If you are in a profession that is exhausting, demanding, physically arduous it needs to be recognized. In these situations, it becomes even more important that you make love choices for your body: what you are eating, breathing, drinking, what you are allowing, how you are resting, and so on.

If your spouse whom you love and have chosen, and who has chosen you, is in a place of uncertainty, insecurity, then they are frightened. They feel not only the financial insecurity; but that you are drifting away, that you are leaving them spiritually and emotionally.

That is not the case. So, both of you: come back to the love. Come back and reexamine together, the love you share. Leave the worries, the financial insecurities, the projected outcomes aside for the moment, and come back to why you are together, that sacred bond. Speak of it on a soul level and on a physical level.

Then decide what you are doing that feels like love and allows you to continue with both the love of partner and the love of your mission and purpose. It does not need to be either/or. Expand your belief about your capacity to do, to be, to receive and create. Change your mindset; choose my choice. You can have it all.

When you feel resistance or blockage in situations, stay in your heart and fill it, and then fill it some more with love. As it breaks open, you may feel that sensation of the ice as it breaks in spring. Allow the sun to continue to warm you and fill you and melt away that resistance.

Resistance is common to many. It is this feeling: "If I open, if I take this quantum leap, if I choose the practicality of love, what if it's not there? What if I say, I open to love, and then I find out that I am not love, I am not loved, and I am not even lovable?" That is the fear. Let it go—give it to me, give it to the Mother, give it to Archangel Michael. Let it go.

What I say to thee, to all of you, is that your construct that you often think of as that spark of light, is the spark of love. It is your essence; it is what you came for. Everything else—the wonderful vessels, the bodies, the situations you have chosen—is window dressing for this unfoldment, for this ascension. Your essence is already there; it is love. Please let it grow.

You are moving past the feeling essence, which is part of your emotional body that is being healed, adjusted, tempered, refined. You are moving to your heart consciousness.

Go to the stillpoint. Go into the depths of your heart, the seat of the soul. Stay there, and throw open your arms and your heart and say, "I receive." I will renew you.

Open To Another Soul

The journey begins with walking the path alone, to the path of union, to the path of joining with All. I come to speak of sacred partnering with your sacred other—with the human beloved one who will walk the Earth with you. This is one of the primary gifts of love.

I do not speak simply of having a friend to spend time with or someone to call partner, husband or wife—for this may or may not be your beloved other. It is time to enter the wholeness of yourself, and from this place of dignity and self-respect, to embrace another in love. It is one of the primary functions of the gift of being human.

Many believe that when I came to this Earth, I walked alone—solitary, with no one by my side. This is incorrect, for I was not monk, priest or rabbi, but a simple man. I did not come into human form to be anything but a simple man and to teach the simple lesson of love. It is befuddling why anyone would think that I would do this without a partner. Yes, there was danger—and protection—for my dear ones, but I did not walk alone.

You cannot truly partner with another unless you have cleared your debris and embraced yourself. I do not mean just the light part of you; I mean all aspects, throughout all time, all reality—not simply what appears in front of you. Walk with me into the darkest corner of your heart, to the dimmest corner of your mind, that you may see what lurks there. You will see that it is simply dust; it is the energy of One, the dust of the universe. It is the very particles of which you are made.

Until you are willing to do this, it is unjust to embrace another. It is unjust to you and it is unjust to that individual—man or woman, angel or alien. I do not mean that you need to become an ascended master before engaging in love, for it is this activity of expansion that will open you further and further. It is the opening to another soul to create the new. It may be in physical form, but it is energy that we speak of. It is love. In this intimate bonding and coming together, you find All—never to be separated yet always to be individual.

Each of you has a sacred flame that burns brightly for another. Some of you rush like moths to the flame, and some of you shield and protect yourselves saying, "You will not invade my sacred space; I must serve." Whom do you serve? If you do not look at your neighbor, your family and your loved ones, you serve no one—not even yourself. When you look at them and open your heart, you serve All.

When you open to another, immediately, instantaneously you increase the energy quotient and grid of love upon this Earth—and that is what you are here to do; it is the restoration. You are being issued an invitation my beloved friends, to open your heart to love. You have opened your heart to my love; what you are asked now to do is to open your heart to another in physical form,

and to partner for life and for the Earth.

These partnerings are not casual. They endure chaos and war; celebration and journey. You are bonding yourself to another forever. Most of you will find that person whom you have already been with for an eternity. Do not turn away. When first I beheld my beloved Mary, it was across a square where I had come to teach and spread my Father's word. Though I believed myself a pious young man, there was nothing calm or pious about my impulse.

You are given these bodies to have this experience, to have your heart race with excitement. In the blending of energy you are given life. It is not about creating life; it is about receiving it. It is about traveling together with a complete honoring of each other's chosen path. There are allowances and compromises, but it is in balance.

I came to Earth to be part of community, to walk with my beloved, to nurture my family, to love and be loved in all ways. I suggest you do the same.

The Nature of Divine Love

I have talked to you many times about how deeply I love you and how grateful I am to have you as part of my family, my life, and my existence. We have traveled together time and time again.

I have told you of my deep love and reverence for my beloved birth parents, the

Universal Mother incarnate and my beloved father Joseph. This has been such a gift, and then to know the joys of kinship with my apostles and disciples; to come to know the joy of marriage and unity of soul, the joy of parenting. These experiences of love, this state of being, of being the incarnation of love has been nothing short of miraculous.

When I say that, I don't mean just for me, I mean for each of you. To have the opportunity to be in a physical form and to know and be love is a gift beyond measure. It is experiencing the essence and energy of One, of the universe, within you, and allowing that to drive, move and fuel you.

Have you never noticed that when you feel out of love whether it is with yourself or another, how you feel flat and out of fuel? But when you are in that love stream, you can conquer mountains, and there is an abundance of energy to go forward and do what your heart desires and to happily share those desires.

One of the things that I have seldom spoken about is the love that I have for those who are on this side with me—for my beloved Father/Mother/One, the Holy Spirit, my beloved Archangels, and those who, like me have come to Earth and worked their way to mastery; which is exactly what you are doing, my friends.

Often, you think of our love as traveling to you, and of course, it does. But it is also embedded within you and then it is reinforced and topped up every millisecond of every day throughout eternity. But I want you to have a glimpse, a sense of the love that we share on this side, among us, as well. This love is so profound and limitless that there is literally nothing that we would not do for each other, that we would not participate in together, that we would not share. It is this place called nirvana. It is the place of bliss, of euphoria, and it is powerful.

The universe is ever expanding, and creation never ceases. That is because the love continues to grow. It isn't fixed, but rather like an ever-expanding balloon which will never burst. We are completely unified, connected, and that connection is in perfect balance. While we are completely One, we also have the delight of our uniqueness. That is part of the creation, just as your uniqueness is part of the creation of Earth.

I love my Mother, your Mother, so deeply that I would always endeavor to do her bidding before she even has the thought. You have this habit of sending each other energy and healing, which is modeled very much on our practice. So if I think that Archangel Michael is working on his Strategic Peace Initiative and could use some reinforcement, I add my energy to him - similarly to Archangel Gabrielle, to my beloved ones, to St. Germaine or Sanat Kumara. It is all equal, unified and balanced.

We do not measure love. You would never hear, "I love you more than her or him or them." It is so expansive, deep, so incredibly wonderful and blissful that the more you give, the more there is to give. It fills you, and it overflows. It moves throughout the universe. That is why love will always reign. It is self-generating, self-perpetuating, and it is the creative force of the universe. Nothing else can do this.

Everything that you are now eliminating on Earth—this sense of separation, of uniqueness being something that has to do with isolation, greed, lust, hate, control—these things do not grow anything.

You ask, "Yeshua, why do you choose today to talk this way to us?" Because we want you to have that same experience, to know we are flooding you. And, we are asking to be flooded by your love. It is when we unite above and below. We wish to witness and participate in the love that you have for each other as well. Flood your planet, expand your field, and join heart to heart.

Emulate us, and let us help. Go with my Love. Go with my blessings. Go with my heart.

The Comfort of Sharing

I am Jesus, brother of your journey and brother of joy. There is much talk these days of crucifixion. I suppose that it is worthwhile, since some may feel better knowing that someone has suffered as much as they. However, for others, it only plagues them.

I want you to know more, not of my pain and suffering, but of my joy and love. That is truly my gift to you. The gift is your ability to walk the Earth knowing you create, heal, speak, and share the words, actions and emotions of love.

There is nothing in any universe, in any creation, that is a greater gift or more important than love. How love expresses itself is in sharing. When you are sad and a friend holds you and pats you on the shoulder, it is the Mother that is being shared. When you are tired and weary and you feel that you cannot take another step, let alone clean the house, and your friend steps forward, and says, "That's okay, I'll do it for you," that is the sharing of the strength and love of the Mother and Father. It is this love from which all is created. That is why we gather together; that we come together in the place of heart and share.

There is no need to struggle in order to ascend—it is to move beyond the mind and into the heart, into the place of feeling, knowing and wisdom. That is what you need do; that is where the creations of love take place.

You are my blessed friends and family; you have comforted me when I have turned to you, and now I come to celebrate life, laughter and miracles. Often you have turned to me and said, "Lord, I wish I could do this and that." Well, now you can. I am anxious to see what you do with this opportunity. You have held it within you and you are birthing it now. It is a birth to be celebrated, for you are birthing your own reality and your own sweet self. I welcome you, and I thank you.

The Jesus Path

I throw open my arms to welcome each and every one of you as I join you on your journey; it is a mutual one. It is a journey of joy and light. It is a journey of unfoldment, mystery, suspense and understanding. It is a shared journey and path; it always has been.

I wish to clarify and share with you what is meant by this term, "The Jesus Path," for it is a catchy little title, but it means so much more.

My disciples, my friends often asked me, "Jesus, how did you do that? How did you multiply bread? How did you heal this individual? How did you make that blind man see? How did you raise Lazarus? How did you...?"

I would tell them, and I tell you today, that I stepped back with the attention of allowing–not intention, but 'attention' of allowing the energy of pure love, of Mother/Father/One, to move through me and to create and co-create.

Why do I use the examples of bread, wine, fish, blind people, and of humans dead and gone? Because the energy and the methods, the strategy, the approach is all the same. I would say then, as I do again today,

"I did not do anything; I allowed." I allowed myself to be the conduit between the Source of One and the molecules of bread, the molecules of man, the molecules of birds. I allowed that union to take place. But it could only take place because the molecules of the bread, the fishes, the loaves, of Lazarus, of the blind were in agreement. They were there saying, "Yes, I will receive. Yes, I will allow. Yes, I truly do wish to fulfill my purpose in a bigger way, a fuller way." For what is the purpose of flour and salt and water except to feed?"

If it had a choice to feed one or two thousand, the choice was clear and in alignment with my mission and purpose. I remind you of this fundamental truth, and of what I said so long ago: "This you will do, and more."

That is what I mean by "The Jesus Path."

It is my agreement to assist, to add my energy, to help you stand back and allow; and for you to be that vessel to bring forth creation and healing and Nova Earth.

The Jesus path isn't that you are following me, my beloved brothers and sisters. It is simply the reminder that I am walking with you. I am not following you and I am not leading you. I am walking with you. There is room enough for both of us, for many of us, for all of us, on this path.

This is not merely the time of ascension. It is you in the fullness of your role as creator, as co-creator; and the acceptance

48

of your role. This is not only part of your ascension; it is the outcome of your ascension. This is not something in the distant future, my beloved ones. It is not something next week or yesterday; it is right now. Yes, we know the reference to "the eternal now" and "being in the present"—and that state of being is critical and essential. When I say, "right now," I mean in your human understanding of the term.

I remember when my Mother would say to me, "Jesus, get in the house right now," I knew what she meant. I say to you, "Can we walk together and create these miracles of healing, of love, of light, of Nova Earth and Nova Being together, right now?"

Bring your attention, intention, and every particle of your being to simply being a conduit. I will help. I will add my energy to you. I will hold your hand, and I am ever present with you.

The Gift of the Sacred Heart of Jesus

I come this day to give you a gift, but I also come to ask you for help.

The mission of this Council of Love is to instill love into the hearts of every being upon this planet, and far beyond. I have no intention of stopping. My human mission, which was cut short, was to instill love and to share the messages of love, freedom and equality.

I come this day and in this moment to share my sacred heart with you. Long ago, I have given my heart to my beloved Magdalena and she to me, but now I wish to give it to you, because that is how deep our connection is.

My capacity for love is infinite; for I am the Son of the Mother/Father/One, as are you. I come this day to give my love to you and to reintegrate and reignite you so you will remember your infinite capacity to love, and pass it on.

Please take my heart, my love, so we can complete our mission which was always about love and the restoration of love. It is not the sacred heart of suffering I offer you, it is the sacred heart of joy. It is the sacred heart of laughter; for when I picked up the children and played or skipped stones across the water, when we made food for thousands or sometimes just for six of us, it didn't matter because it was being human and family.

Help me in this completion and in this ascension. I know your hearts, and I know the answer is 'Yes.' Allow me to complete this overlighting within you.

You shine brighter than the sun on the water. You shine deeply into the depths.

Thank you. We will never be separated again. Go with my love, and go with my heart.

CHAPTER 3
LOVE YOUR
SACRED SELF

You have perfected forgiveness and love of your brothers and sisters, but it is time that you perfected it for your sacred self as well. You turn to me and you say, "I'm doing well on that." Well, you have just begun.

I know what it is to be a human being—to have those moments and mornings when you look in the mirror and think, "Who do you think you are? What on Earth are you doing here?" I am here with you this day, as I have been with you forever, to be the face and eyes that look back at you in the mirror. So when you ask that question you will hear the truth: that you are me; that you are the heart of God; that you are the messenger of the universe.

You have come in sacred purpose which has entailed sacrifice; never think this is not known and recognized. You have known moments of despair and sacrifice.

Don't think we are beyond emotion; that is a human construct. Our emotion is of a different nature that is beyond comprehension. We hold you in sacred regard. Our love for you is bigger than this planet, bigger than this universe; even your smallest kernel of concern is known.

Let me speak of this opening of the portal, this energy that descends upon the Earth right now. It is a cosmic doorway. What you are doing is opening the portals of your heart wider than you have ever done before, in joy and recognition of who you are and who you are to each other.

As you do this you are holding open the curtains, tearing down the veils, to allow the full impact of the energy that is coming to Earth at this time to be felt. Yes, the door will open no matter what. The last time around, when I was born, the full impact was not felt. You have volunteered to make sure that this time and at this place, on this planet, it will be.

It is a gift to you and it is a gift to us—and we thank you, knowing that completion is ensured.

As I have walked the Earth I have not walked alone, and neither do you. We walk together as trusted friends. Now is a time of stepping forward. And again, I do not do so alone. I do so with you, my brothers and sisters, as we have stepped forward time and time again. We do so in the speaking of truth, and in the healing and holding of the light.

Do not think that you are alone, you aren't. You might as well throw open the door and put out the welcome mat, because I am with you.

How Can I Help?

I wish to say I believe in you. I always have. I wish to speak to you this day from the bottom of my being about what you are doing on Earth at this time. I do not come with prophecies, and I do not come with a history lesson and reminders of when I have walked with you, as I have often done. I come to speak to you about your hearts, about living in this present moment, and how I live there with you always.

Many of you have ideas of or experiences with me, for many of you have been with me when I had incarnated as Yeshua and in other times and realms as well. I could also speak to those realms of the future when we will walk together yet again, and I am looking forward to it.

I honor the Mother's plan, for I do not return in physical form to Earth to a place that is war torn. But that does not mean I am not completely and always present with you. I have chosen to be in what you think of as spirit form. Sometimes you think it's because that is the easiest and most blissful of all, that I can sit in the ecstasy. That is not why I am in this form. I am in this form because it gives me access to each of your hearts, your minds and your bodies, these wonderful temples that you have created.

One of the reasons I am in this form is that I can be ever present, ever helpful, ever loving with you. I am not some distant deity. I am the brother of your heart and soul, and I am as much a part of your family and circle as the person sitting next to you.

Previously, in fact many times, our Mother has asked you to step forward in the brilliance and the truth of who you are; to stop hiding in the shadows. I repeat that plea. And you are doing it. But sometimes you say to me, "Well, Yeshua, I feel a little

nervous and conspicuous, and my family thinks I'm crazy." And I say to you, your family loves you, your family above and below love you.

Let us be very clear, there is no greater treasure above or below than your family. And some of you have not been blessed with the fulfillment of the dream that you had when you joined your family or when you birthed your family. But I want to remind you in this moment and in this life and in this time, you do have a family—right here. You have strangers and acquaintances and dear friends who love you and see you for the truth and the wonder of who you are.

This is what I want to assist you with in this present moment. Yes, I am asking you: Step forward and get going. And while you are doing that, can you simply relax and be? Can you be the totality of who you are? Can you allow and strip away these various personas? They only hide you, and there is no need for hiding. You are magnificent just the way you are. Let go of all artifice. Let go of the belief that you need to be one way or another.

My Magdalena used to laugh at me when I would get full of myself or become too serious, and she would say, "Who do you think you are, the savior?" And we would laugh, realizing that regardless of what the path or job or mission or sacred contract is, that all I really had was that moment with my wife and family to laugh and to help with supper, to sit and talk, or simply watch the children play.

So this is what I am asking of you. This is my sacred request. In the very moment, each and every time you breathe, I am asking to be with you. Not as teacher, not as savior, not as prophet, but as beloved friend and brother, here to help. Here to help and nudge you along, and remind you of the sacred space that you are. Not the sacred space that you are becoming, but the very sacred space that you are. The essence of your being flows so beautifully, your love is so clear and brilliant, that I want to be next to you.

Often you think of us as directing, and that is not so. We are in genuine partnership. We are of the same family, so you can ask me, please ask me, to help in different ways, to support you in ways that you need. Not the convoluted, "Please support me in doing this because I am doing God's work." You can leave the second half off—I know what you're up to. I want to support you, and I want to sit with you.

I want to sit and join you with the Buddha and simply be. In physicality you cannot constantly be jumping and stepping, skipping, dancing forward and not take time to simply be. It is essential work to take time to refill. I wish to walk next to you for hundreds of years if that is your choice, so don't cut your life short. Be in the balance of stillness, action and laughter. Let the tears you cry be the tears of joy.

There has been far too much misery upon this planet of love. It makes no sense. How does that shift? It changes by you standing back prior to and after being in the melee, and allowing the refill. And when I say refill, I also mean reflection, perspective, evaluation and feedback. I want to be having that conversation with you. How is it going? And how can I help?

You are the preparers of the way. There are times when you feel that this is hard and that you are alone. I suggest you look around your circle and remember in form who is gathered. But also know that in between each and every one of your circle, there are dozens trying to sneak their way in to be with you. They are not just the ones that you call saints or prophets or masters. There are so many throughout the multiverse who wish to assist in this time of transformation. I do not say this casually. This isn't about calendars. This is about journeys and the collective transforming how they think and perceive.

You have had terrible experiences on Earth where you have witnessed people who have been mind-controlled or programmed. Healing to remove that programming prematurely can be destructive and harmful, because it can be a subtle method of self protection. Part of that subtle programming is what you say to yourself, my beloved ones. So the healing and transformation is literally letting go of all those programs and preconceptions; of simply, fully and completely anchoring in your body and upon the planet. Right here, right now. I talk to you about the now because that is what we have together, and the now is eternal.

The transformation that is finally taking place upon this planet is nothing short of miraculous, and it is miraculous my brothers and sisters because of you. You think that you are not highly effective.

You have grown your energy field a thousandfold in incorporating what you read this day. Think of this. You were already big, and now you have expanded even further. Is it any wonder that we ask, that I ask from my heart to yours, to be with you, to hang out with you in a love-in? It is all there is— love. It is all there ever has been. It's all I ever talk about. I am surprised people are even still listening. It's repetitive. And yet it is the one thing I know to be true.

Please, let me be with you. I do not wish and I will not dictate to you what that looks like. I would like us to discuss it—you and I, quietly. Tell me how you wish me to be with you. Tell me how you want me to communicate to you, in what areas you really want me to help you, and in what areas you think, "I'm doing fine. Just back off." Just tell me.

And then listen to what I have to contribute to our conversation. But do not jump forward. You may glance back, but do not go back. You can't anyway. Stay in this moment and be with me and be with our family. Farewell.

Who Are You?

Welcome, my beloved friends, brothers and sisters all. Welcome to this time of reunion, of transformation, of recovery and rediscovery. What is it rediscovery of, my beloved ones? It is rediscovery of your sacred self. I have been sitting here and repeating again and again, "Who are you? Who are you?" because I want you, I invite you, I beg you, to remember the fullness of who you really are.

Many of you think of yourselves as humans, as masters in the making, as angels or archangels. But, my beloved friends, you are all of these things and so much more.

What I invite you to do this day is to come back, not only to your angelic self, but also to the truth, back to the time when you were sheer energy, a pure light being.

Come with me now, without form, knowing that part of you is eternal. That spark of light, that touch of love, has anchored within you as an angel and human being; It is important now that as you transcend dimensions and realities, and claim your new journey, that you clear about who you are.

Many of you turn to me and say, "I don't see, I don't know, I don't understand." Go back beyond your angelic self or before your other adventures. Go to that spark of light of who you really are. I know you; I have always known, loved, cherished and honored you. But I want you to know yourself.

So many times you ask, "Jesus, where are you? When are you going to show up? How can I see you? How can I sit with you?" I understand and share this yearning. This day, my beloved ones, I am asking you to come and sit in your purity and essence—the clarity of who you are—with me. I am that magenta spark of light right next to you.

Your Eternal Tri-Flame

Welcome my beloved family, brothers and sisters of my heart, of my tri-flame, for this is a pattern that is carried throughout, not only in what you think of as spirit form but throughout all life, all reality, and all species.

Have you ever considered the tri-flame of your favorite dog or cat or monkey? Have you thought of the tri-flame of Gaia and how brightly it burns to support and warm you?

Allow me this brief discussion about the tri-flame. You have many words for death: the body transitions, a person dies, expires or passes. But what is it except a laying down of the form, of the body that you have chosen to travel with throughout a lifetime. When you die your tri-flame does not expire, the tri-flame goes with you; it is infinite and eternal, as clear and brilliant as your beautiful snowflake soul design. It is singularly unique to you.

I mention this about your soul design and about your tri-flame because so often

when one dies, whether it is from what you term 'natural causes', which very often are quite unnatural; or from tragedy, there is grieving, a sense of loss that that person or group that you have known or may not even have known personally is gone. My beloved friends, yes, the body is gone but the soul, the tri-flame, the soul design never dies, it never leaves, it continues on.

Your unique soul design and tri-flame does not change from lifetime to lifetime to lifetime. It is eternal and infinite. It is how you are known and recognized throughout the universe. You have had many bodies, many forms, some beautiful and some not; for every size and shadow, every pair of shoes and hat has been tried on. That journey is what has brought you to this place of mastery, to this place of wisdom.

Always keep your tri-flame of the divine feminine of blue diamond, the divine masculine of gold diamond, and your unique pink diamond burning brightly, vibrantly. It is one of the ways in which we see you, and more importantly how you may see, know and love your sweet self.

You Are the Innocent Lamb

Brothers and sisters of my heart and my soul, it is the time of Spring, of new beginnings. I ask each of you to think of yourself as a lamb; a newborn, ready to frolic in the meadows and open to nurturing. Each of you has need of replenishment; you have asked, and you are thirsty. You wish to know your sacred selves, and in that embrace, to know All.

It is time my dear ones, to perform your miracles of love, to awaken self within. You do this, not as mature adult but as the innocent lamb, the butterfly, and the sweet flowers of Spring. We have much to do together in laughter and play, in rebirth of the Mother Earth, in rebirth of self, in rebirth of many of us who will walk this planet with you. It is the rebirth of love incarnate. It is the recognition that you have been born to walk this place in unity, connectedness and balance, in laughter, in play. You have come to be Spirit having a physical experience; nothing more and nothing less.

Give me your woes; I will cast them out to the thin air and return to you sunshine. Walk with me, for I am with you.

The Illusion of Lack of Self Worth

You gather in the name of unity and in the name of love, and when you do so, much is accomplished. You change the face of the planet. You hold her together, and much is prepared.

I do not wait to visit you. I am busy about my Father's business and shall be among you soon. Take this as you please; it does not matter. Physical form has always been questioned amongst my followers, amongst my brothers and sisters. But let there be no doubt that I am with you

physically, and that I am with each of you to dismiss this illusion regarding worth. Long ago, in a moment of despair, I questioned my own worth as a human and man, and I have seen and felt how destructive such feelings are, how terrible.

I will assist you, not to make the world safe for me, but so that you may join and travel the universe freely, in laughter and love, without fear of separation, retribution or judgment. Limitation is not your inheritance. The gift of life was freely given to you, without limitations. You need only enjoy it. Come with me and celebrate, for we are indeed all one.

The sense of unworthiness is equivalent to the human fall from grace, and Archangel Gabrielle is the major conciliator between the forces harboring this negative effect. As many of the angels fell, they embraced the sense of ego that they were "greater than," and this was ludicrous. And you, my sweet brethren, embraced the illusion that you were "less than". The sense of unworthiness that the human race has felt has been, in one sense, your own darkness. It's time for the light to overtake it, to incorporate it into love and wholeness.

One day we will sit and watch the sun set. You may hold me to this. It will be our time and it will be in this time.

Your Real Mission

I come with eagerness, excitement, awe and wonder to share with you more deeply and fully the patterning of the universe, the patterning of the Mother—which is the patterning of your construction, your experience, your expression, and the expression of All.

There is a dichotomy here because, on the one hand, you are absolutely unique; your soul design, the beauty and wonder of who you are is singular in the entirety of the universe, the multiverse, the omniverse. Throughout all galaxies, all planets, all realities, all dimensions, you are a unique expression of the Mother, the Father and the One. There is no other you. On the other hand, in this dichotomy, all things—all life, all energy, all form, all non-form, all existence—is patterned upon the Mother. The pattern of the Mother is in all things. Through her breath She has created all things.

Is this not magnificent? It doesn't matter whether you conceive of yourself as human, angelic, archangel, fairy or cherubim. The range of expressions is infinite, far more than you know. But the entire point is: All forms, all realities, all sense of beingness—whether a tree, stone or mountain, frog or fairy, or human—all are patterned by, with and through the Divine Mother.

You are not merely a spark of divinity. Your entirety is of the pattern of the Divine Mother/Father/One. It is not just a spark to

be ignited. It is your teeth, jaw, bones, liver; it is your outer auric fields. It is the entirety of your being above and below, within and without.

There is a part of you that has remained out of form, as sheer energy, which also has the same patterning and your unique design. You have come with a mission and purpose to this beautiful planet, this archangel called Gaia, for two things—just like I did as Jesus. Let us approach this as brothers and sisters.

You came for two reasons; both are the fulfillment and unfoldment of the Mother's Plan and Design. First and foremost, your mission is to be love, to know love, to express love, and to know and be joy. This is your primary mission before you do anything else—before you attend to the tedious matters of life, whether it is health, taxes, feeding a family or keeping a roof over your head. Your first, primary job is to be, know and express love—and to do so in such a way that you are in infinite joy. There are many gradations of joy. In its simplest form, it is not merely being happy. Happy is reactive; you are happy about something. Joy is a state of being; it is your birthright and it is the essence of the Mother. The Mother is not neutral; She is explosive, outrageous and indescribable joy.

That is the first part of your mission. Then, when you are anchored in the love—the love of your beautiful, sacred self, of the wonder of your unique design that is an

absolute physical embodiment of the pattern of One, of Source—you move into the expression and the experience of that love.

With this comes the experience and expression of your mission: what you discussed with the Mother, with us, and your guides and guardians prior to return, about what you wanted to do and how you felt you could assist the Mother in the fulfillment of this beautiful Plan.

But first comes the joy, because you cannot fully complete your mission and purpose if you are in agony, pain and sorrow, grief, or lack.

The expression of your mission and purpose, in terms of action, needs to be joyful. If it is done with a sense of, "I better do what I promised," a sense of drudgery, or a sense of, "I am afraid I am not good enough," then it is not of divinity or the truth of who you really are. The Mother did not say to me, or to any of you, "Go down to Earth, and see how much you can endure. If you're really good at endurance and if you finally surrender, I'll give you a prize and you can come home." That would not be of love.

It is time, my beloved friends, once and forever to get rid of this sense of endurance—even in situations that may appear as filled with obstacles, challenging or difficult to see within.

Stop Lying to Yourself

I bring you the desert rose this day. I collected them as I ventured away into retreat, to find the silence of my soul and the voice of my being. When the internal and external noise get too loud, it is important to venture out into the desert, into your place of sacred retreat, and to refind the silence of your being.

There are times when the noise comes simply from everyday life. It does not need to be chaos; it can simply be the busyness of the human experience, and that is part of the joy as well. But when the busyness and the noise tips into irritation, interference or static, then know it is time to come and walk with me in the desert. It is time to smell the air of purity, to know it is the purity of your own being, and to find the desert rose that grows wild. In the most barren of places beauty thrives, and it thrives within you—it always has.

Many of you ask when will I return and walk with me on Earth? When will you come and share my dinner? When may I host you and tend to you like the brother you are?"

The promise is clear; I will return. But my promise to the Mother as well is that I will return in peace and in the time of the Golden Age. Archangel Michael has made tremendous strides towards peace on Earth. As he does, and as each of you works with your sacred chores—hether it is in Iraq or

Afghanistan, the Middle East or the White House; your communities or your families; massive change is being anchored.

The world may look and smell like upheaval; it is very noisy and very loud. There are many who are simply speaking for the joy of hearing their own voice. But that is all it is, noise. Ignore what is not truth.

You know exactly what I am talking about. Truth is a stand alone quality, an interdimensional gift. But truth, like joy, is embedded within you as well; it lives fiercely in your heart and in your bones. So when you hear untruth, when you witness untruth, it is very clear because not only does it not resonate with the divine wisdom, it does not resonate with you.

I wish to be bold with you this day; I wish for you to hear in your heart what I say to you. I preface it by telling you how deeply I love you and honor you. But there are times when you lie to yourself.

Oh, I do not mean the grand lie of living a lie. But there are times when you simply enter denial and are far from truthful with yourself. Sometimes it is out of dreaming and self protection; even though you know the truth, you tend to look the other way. I would do this from time to time with my beloved Mary and my beautiful daughter, Sarah.

I would say to myself, No, it's going to be all right. I will be here to shield them, defend them, watch my daughter grow and to watch our love grow. I would know I was lying to myself; I was making noise. It's not that it was harmful, but it was not consistent with the truth of my being. Each of you falls into this pattern at times.

This shouldn't make you feel less than, or as chastisement. All I want you to do is to acknowledge when you are lying to yourself.

Each of you has an incredibly magnificent plan. I have asked you to step forward in service. Do not lie to yourself thinking that you are doing as much as you possibly can. You are such expanded, magnificent beings that there is always more.

I am not asking, guiding, or suggesting that you go over the top and make yourself ill. When I ask you to step forward, I ask you to step forward in joy and completion of who you are, to let the human race see who you are—teachers and healers and my disciples, my best friends. So don't lie to yourself, you are "more than."

When you need to hide away and find the silence, come with me; it is essential. Then I will say to you, "Now, let's go back full force and be who we are." Until the day I walk with you in physical form, I will walk with you in spirit; I will inspire you, and I will help you balance so you don't go off on wild goose chases.

It is in the silence that the truth is known and heard; then you bring it forth and allow the rose blossom. You are the truth. You are the anchors and the beacons. It is time to acknowledge the fullness of that; it is time to awaken the human race.

I honor you, I respect you, and I know what you are capable of. Grand gestures happen every day, and I do not mean in the United Nations, the White House, Paris or Rome. They happen on the beach, talking to a friend; they happen in extending healing to someone in need. It happens with your family in tolerance and love, and it happens by looking in the mirror.

Do not underestimate who you are. If you do, I will remind you; there is no room for doubt, and there is no room for lies. Give the Mother your doubt and give me your lies. And we will give you back love, complete acceptance, and a clear reminder of who you are.

Go with my love and go in absolute silent peace.

Claim Your Dreams

You are my bringers and holders of compassion and vision. You do the work and creation of Nova Earth and you do so because you are Nova Beings. You have come from the past, the future and the now and you carry within you all codes, all knowing, all love, all sweetness.

Do not doubt yourself; do not doubt your ability, capacity and gifts. They are not only what you think of as divinely given; they are also, my beloved ones, self pro-

claimed and self claimed. You brought them with you, and they are stored, like seeds, in the blessed infinity and essence of your heart.

I come this day to ask you, and to remind you, to be true to yourself, know yourself.

Knowing yourself is not only of the sweetness of your heart, but of the dreams, the desires of what you wish to create—for your sweet self, your family, your soul family and this journey back to One—in this life, in this time, in this body, and by this name.

Do you know yourself? Are you being absolutely honest, forthright, diligent and vigilant? Are you digging deep and then deeper into what you truly desire?

This invitation is not a fool's errand. Too often as I walk, sit and even dine with you, I feel and hear and see your dreams; I see what you wish to create in both the personal ways (which you think of as smaller), and in the global ways.

Too often I hear you censure yourself, thinking, "That isn't possible," or "That will never happen," or "I don't believe that will happen." Those statements, as subtle as they are, are statements of lack of self-worth, lack of self love, and limitation of your creative power.

Let me be practical. You say, "Jesus, I yearn for a sacred union relationship where I am free to express my heart, thoughts, moods and my most secret dreams without fear. I will join with another to bring forth not only what I desire, but what they desire." Then you add, "Oh, I can't even meet somebody; how is that ever going to happen? I'd better let that go."

Or you dream of a home, a sacred space; not a mansion in the sky but a place that is in nature, where the birds, bees, bunnies and foxes all are with you—even the coyotes, the mountain lions, the bears and deer. A home anchored upon the heart-space of Gaia, where there is a place for your altar, and a table to share food, laughter and nourishment of every description with friends. Then I hear you say, "Oh, I barely have money for rent. I can't do that." Then you let it go.

What I am asking of you this day is to have extraordinary courage; to have the courage to truly not only explore your dreams, your desires, of what you choose to bring forth—but also to have the courage to claim your dreams.

You are extraordinary in working for world peace, for an end to drought, for an end to war, persecution, mayhem and chaos. All these things you work to destroy in order to bring forth the new. And, dear hearts, you are stellar at this.

I could bring you kudos from Archangels Michael, Raphael, Uriel and Gabrielle, and far beyond. What I ask of you, because I love you, because I cherish you, is to have the courage to explore the dreams of your heart. Don't let them go.

When I was incarnated, I and my Magdalena knew we had a mission and purpose. But the dream of my heart was also to know love, to be in partnership, to have a family, to have my circle of friends so we could break bread together. People think of the Last Supper, but what they forget is it was every supper.

How often we gathered in fellowship and mutuality, laughter and support. It was not heavy; laughter, dreaming, sharing is sacred. It is what builds unity and community; it is what builds Nova Earth.

I ask you "Are you true to yourself or do you negate yourself?" Honor who you are. These desires and dreams are not placed within your heart to torture you; they are guideposts, they are signage along the way to show you which way to turn.

If you do not start with a dream, you are denying yourself. This makes it difficult for us to co-create with you. When you are in the clarity of who you are, your purpose and what you intend to bring forth, everything is possible.

I will help you. Let go of the fear of limitations, and let's explore the depths of your dreams.

Freedom

You are the activators of the future and the now. And we, the company of Heaven, are here as your reinforcements.

"Embrace each morning
as a resurrection."

I have repeatedly said you are far ahead of schedule in terms of what you think of as the anchoring of the Mother's Plan upon Gaia.

You say to me, "Jesus, it sure doesn't feel that way." But look around. Pay attention to what is being created as never before. You are creating anew and it starts with your beautiful sacred self. It starts with the deep acknowledgement and acceptance of the entirety of your being; the homecoming to your soul. You have need, my beloved ones, not only to glimpse and see, but to whole-heartedly embrace the truth of who you are: the totality of your power, gentleness, vision and strength. It is neither coincidence nor accident that you are here at this time.

I speak about freedom. I mean freedom in every sense of the word. I know the experience of free choice, of free will. It is a blessing beyond belief; it is a sacred trust from the Mother and Father of All.

Freedom means many things. When I walked the Earth it was the freedom to align with my Mother and Father's plan of unfoldment. I was the one who planted the seeds of love, but you are the harvesters. We want to share the joy of the bounty of the harvest with you.

Let me talk in practical terms about free-dom. It is freedom from want, from strug-gle, from desires not met. It is freedom from illusion, from chaos, political, economic, social, familial and communal. I know of these things. There were many who wished

me to embrace the chaos of the political situation, but it did not serve.

And so I give you this gift of freedom, so claim this birthright of freedom just as I have. Freedom to simply be the truth of who you are.

This freedom entails choices, creations, by each of you. Do not turn to me and say, "Lord, I do not know how to create," for that is simply not so. You are creating reality with every breath, with every in and out breath that you take. And if you are con-fused about how to do so, then I am with you. I am not with you as a distant entity; I am with you as your closest friend and ally. Yes, I have promised the Mother that I will not take form until such time as there is peace, but peace is very close at hand. It is much closer than any of you can believe. It will occur in miraculous ways. The time of conflict, whether it is interpersonal or global, is over.

It is a decree that each one of you is sending out, because there is no freedom in struggle, war, poverty, hunger, strife, death and disease. It is the time of awakening, and it is the time of declaring your personal free-dom. I would say I gave it to you, but really, you already had it. I request of you that you declare and live your freedom. Do the little things that have to be done or adjusted to live your joy – that is freedom.

I never ask of you to do your service in such ways that it drags you down, makes your heart heavy, makes you feel like you are carrying the cross; this is not what we are asking. Throw off the yoke. Allow us to help. We are your team, as you are ours. I welcome you home to Terra Gaia. I welcome you home to my heart.

Invitation to Resurrection

I share my passion and compassion with each and every one of you this day. I want to talk about resurrection, of rebirth and of new beginnings, of anchoring and ascension—and how you find your balance right in the middle. I come to you as brother and friend, and I come to you as Master of Love, as bringer of love.

You have done miraculous work, and have been tried and true. You have been honest and honorable. And you've had your dark nights of the soul just as I have. But you also awaken to a bright new day.

Did you ever wonder what it was I did between my physical death and resurrection? There have been many myths that have said that I did not die upon the cross. I can assure you it was not fast but I most certainly died. My physical life ended.

Does my soul die? Does my spirit die? Not ever.

Did you ever wonder what I did between Friday and Sunday? Did I just sort of lie there waiting? During that time, I was present. I was lifted up—what you may think of as initial ascension—and was bathed, com-

pletely returned into the love. I had the joy, the experience, of returning into and being the love.

As human man, I was fortunate that the veil did not exist for me. I knew who I was, and I knew the carrying of love, the sharing of love, and that I was loved and lovable. I knew my mission and purpose for the Mother—my Mother and your Mother—was the reanchoring of love. That didn't mean I was not human; that I did not have moments of fear, angst, anger, frustration or joy, or happiness, which is different than joy. I did. But during that hiatus on sweet Saturday, I became once again, one with love.

Often you think of love, but you do not think of what it truly is. You describe it through an attribution of the Divine Qualities: love is joy, love is peace, love is compassion, love is truth. All this is true. Or, you describe it as you love somebody, that you are loved, that you have experienced love, that you love God, that God loves you, the Mother loves you, I love you. There is a lot of back and forth in this love.

When I say that I reentered the love, what I mean is that I re-merged with Mother/Father/One/Source, Allah, Yahweh—whatever you think of as the One. What is love? It is Source—it is the essence, the All of the Mother/Father/One.

I died to achieve that reunion, and you, my beloved ones, have been given this gift of love in the gift of the 13th Octave. I remind you of that. Yes, there is the seventh dimension of love, what I think of sometimes as "home base," but if you truly want to be reunited, to be the love—take my hand and come with me to the 13th Octave.

Why do I speak of this, of what I was up to on that infamous Saturday?

Because, my beloved ones, it is very parallel to what you have been, and are, doing. Yes, you have cleared; you have been washed, cleaned, and filled with the Mother's love, with Her essence, with the experience of love. She has planted that very love within you; She has germinated it. That is what is going on now, but the seed was planted eons ago.

You have done your ascension into the love. You have done your descent in the anchoring and integration of love: the allowing of the flowering, the germination of the seed, the anchoring of the Divine Qualities, the anchoring of the experience of love. You are ready to fully anchor and descend into form—like I have in returning to that body lying in Joseph of Arimathea's tomb.

Why would I be able to ascend into Heaven? Because I was the Son of One? Not exactly. I could ascend because I was rejoined, filled, completed and reunited; I became the purity of love yet again.

The Mother has given you the gift of the purity. Like me, you are ready to ascend – not to leave this beloved planet that I so dearly cherish. Frankly, I can't wait to return to walk with you, break bread with you, and laugh with you!

Your ascension does not mean that you have to leave, that you take your body and go home. The Mother is not calling to you the same way she called to me to return home. Your ascension, your resurrection, your rebirth—is more miraculous than mine. You remain on sweet Gaia as the love, as the divinity of who you are, of the totality of all your aspects, all your talents—awakened.

When I return, I will choose to have a similar, although updated, look so that you will recognize me as Jesus, but I will not be that same man that lived thousands of years ago. You have the opportunity—the invitation, the energy, the entire realm of the love—to be in form, to continue on.

As brother and friend, as one who loves you so deeply, I invite you to your resurrection. Will you join me? I will take you when you're ready, but the invitation is for right now: to bathe yourself, to join with the love, and awaken tomorrow reborn.

Practice Resurrection Every Day

I wish to speak to you further about resurrection. I do not mean resurrection in the religious, traditional sense; I mean the resurrection of each of us.

Many of you think of the word resurrection in terms of my death and departure, and there is a sadness related to this at times. It is the sadness and feeling of loss that I wish to erase—not only in terms of your relationship to me, but in relationship to yourself and to each other.

Dear hearts, this is a time of resurrection. Note that I am not using the term "ascension," because between now and then, there are many resurrections. You are traveling at the speed of love, to higher and higher frequencies. In this, you are experiencing what you can think of as many deaths, as you leave the old behind.

Many of you have thought that your memories are becoming dim. Perhaps you are suffering from dementia or Alzheimer's, because you are failing to remember what you are leaving behind. What I say to you is, what you are leaving behind is insignificant. There is no need, no requirement, no desire to remember pain, suffering, sorrow, angst, anger, despair, disappointment. None of that has any place within your expanded, resurrected self.

You tend to think of resurrection as death and going home, back to the heart of Mother/Father/One. But do you not do this each and every day as you travel to the 13th Octave? You carry that within your hearts, your minds and your physical form.

I am guiding you to embrace each morning as a resurrection. When you fall asleep, you leave behind the previous day, week, month, year—letting it die in terms of passing from you. Don't carry its debris forward. That includes the night work that

you do with Archangels Michael, Raphael, Gabrielle, Jophiel and Uriel. It includes the healing taking place at night. It includes any sense of burden. Then, you begin each day anew with the rebirth, not only of your sacred self, but of awe, wonder, potential and love.

You ask, "Jesus, why are you suggesting rebirth rather than expansion?" What I am saying to you is that rebirth does expand.

When a new child, a new soul, is born unto the world there is a sense of the miraculous. There is the sense of wonder, of heart-opening and joy when one gazes at the purity and beauty of a newborn baby—even when the baby is desperately ugly, as many new babies are. But that ugliness, in terms of your definition of beauty, is always overlooked because it is so miraculous. The sweetness and the bravery, the valor and courage of this being to come to the planet and to share with you, to be with you, is such a gift. Even if it is only a new baby passing by in the grocery store, in the market, it is a gift to your heart. If you hear them cry, it immediately brings out this sense of wanting to comfort and cherish.

This is what I am asking: To see yourself, to be as gentle and sweet and in such profound awe of yourself as we are of you. Each and every day, commit to your resurrection: to being in physical form, having been reborn directly from the heart of One.

It is time to rediscover awe; that sense of joy, of amazement of being on Gaia. It's the sense of love you have for our Mother that you would do this. Know each day, we are holding you in our arms, swaddling you, coddling you, loving you. Farewell.

Being in the State of Forgiving

I come to speak to you this day about forgiving. Not forgiveness, but forgiving as an action. As you advance and expand into the wonderful wholeness of your mighty self, your capacity to stay in the heart of forgiving is infinite.

Being in the state of forgiving is critical and part of the shift to the place of love. When you live in the place of love, you finally acknowledge and fully embrace that love is all you are, all you ever have been, and all you ever will be. That does not eliminate the need for forgiving.

You are divine perfection and in that, you are having a wonderful human experience. That does not mean there will never be a misstep. There is the one you love, or a neighbor, or someone who is in the process of awakening, who will do, say or project something that is unloving which requires forgiveness. This is why, my dear friends, I ask you to stay in the constant state of forgiving.

Many of you have let go of expectations and judgments of others; you have done a magnificent job. Yet you still have expectations of yourself: how you wish to proceed, what you wish to achieve, what stepping forward means, how you wish to behave, how you wish not to behave. You find fault with yourself as you seek the corners until you find that speck of self-blame.

But when you remain in the place of forgiving—in the heart center of forgiving—you are able also to forgive your sweet self and to see it in the light of the expansion that it is, to see it as bringing to light something that you wish to expand into. Rather than perceiving it as lack, recognize it is expansion.

If there is a corner that is shadowy or dark and you explore it with the heart of forgiving—of being in that state of Oneness—then you can proceed without being afraid that you're going to be at fault. And similarly you can approach the world, the collective, the populace because you are in that place of forgiving.

It is not something that I am asking you to drift in and out of. It is not a ten-year-old having a fight and saying, "then I will forgive you," yet remembering it for the rest of your life. It is a state of being; it is the state of being forgiving just as you are in the state of being love. They are synonymous and they are inseparable, like hope and trust.

You are in the midst of massive change— more significant and massive than most of you are even dreaming of. It is not cataclysmic; it is miraculous, it is expansive. But in that change, if fear arises and you are in the place of forgiving, you forgive the fear and you reassure it.

If people are assuming certain scenarios and you bring forgiving to it this dissipates the energy. Forgiving is one of the cornerstones of being able to live in and be part of the collective.

There is much that has gone forward, in this life and others, both on and off planet. Forgiving does not eliminate the memory; what it does is put it in perspective and not only allows you but encourages you, moves you along as does a current in a stream.

Forgiveness of self is all important. Toward the end of my life there were moments when I was very harsh with myself because I felt that I had not completed what I came here to do. And my beloved Magdalena would turn to me and say, "Jesus, you must forgive yourself. You cannot go on or go forward or complete your journey unless your heart is forgiving, and forgiving of self." Then she would tease me and say, "Who do you think you are, God?" And we would laugh.

I say this to you in the same way that my beloved has said it to me, "Who do you think you are, God?" The answer to that is, "Yes, of course you are." You are the infinite spark and the unique expression of One. Because of that you are the embodiment of infinite forgiving.

Allow this quality to come forward as never before. We know that there are times that you wail at heaven, that you are angry or upset with your guides. We are not deaf. You feel that your guardians have not delivered in a timely manner; they have not made you have this or that experience. But their wisdom and their understanding of your unfoldment is greater than your own. Never do we seek to override your free will, but there are times when we will hold back so that you may make those choices appropriately.

We also ask you in the state of forgiving to look at the entirety of the universe. It is about wiping the slate clean and keeping the slate clean, particularly for your sweet self.

If you are having difficulty in staying in this place of forgiving, which is compassion, then turn to me. I will be there. I have always been with you; I am not about to walk away now.

Forgive all ideas that you have about yourself and what you have or have not accomplished or experienced in this lifetime. Let's begin once again to walk together in love. Go with my blessings, go with my peace—and go with my laughter.

Addiction & Forgiveness

Many families follow patterns of addiction. It is important for you and all beings to understand the differences between addiction and balance. Many of you have freed yourself from a family pattern of addiction. All addictions are addictions to pain; it is the pain and the ability to try to numb the pain that results in abuse of drugs, sex, gambling and alcohol. Then, it becomes a physical need, but that is not really the crux of the matter.

I also remind you that one of my first acts was to create wine for the celebration of matrimony in Cana of Galilee. It was in balance. In physical form you are given gifts, whether it is delicious food that nourishes your body or excites your senses, or a sip or cup of wine; this is not detrimental to your process of ascension.

It is the process of addiction that is detrimental to ascension. Your physical body is undergoing massive change. Because of this, you need to be vigilant about what you are putting in your form and welcoming into your field. If it is excessive "anything," it is going to interfere with the flow of energy.

You may often think that your family members have not followed your release, but look to the upcoming generation; that is where you are teaching and where your example is truly being anchored. They are seeing that there are choices.

You are seeing so many people in turmoil because this issue of pain and addiction is being brought to the surface. This is not as an act of punishment or cruelty, but rather as an opportunity for release. It has already begun; which is why, my beloved friends, that sometimes it is very important to stand back and be the observer. Enter discernment, erect your shields if necessary, and send love, support and light. Don't allow the chaos to invade your sacred space.

Food is another area that many are engaged in emotional eating. It's an addiction. You are hungry for love. What you are doing is asking for help with control of the food issue. Give away, over and over again, the issue of food. We will take it! But what you also need to start with, is to eat love. Think of the balance.

You ask, "how on earth do I eat love?" There's a secret. Eat green, breathe green, and bring in a touch of pink and red as well. Change how you think about food; this is true for all of you. This is the Nova Being, this is the New You. Not in a flamboyant manner, but in a very quiet private manner, pray over your food or drink, or whatever you are putting in your body. In that prayer, transmute anything that is not of wholeness that is not for your highest good; simply transmute it into love.

Be cognizant and take that moment before you put something in your body. Look at it, whether it is in your hand, on a napkin or plate, in a pot or in a carton and ask, "Does this food look like love?" If the answer is yes, then eat it. Be honest with yourself. If the answer is no, then set it aside.

If you are in transition, add more green. Even if it is a bowl of ice cream, partner it with a bowl of salad. The color of green is the color of love; it is the ray of love. If you do this, you will see that your struggle will cease. Be very conscious with yourself: "I am giving away the addiction—and I am eating, smoking, drinking, ingesting love."

Remember, the worst judgment you can ever receive is the judgment you pass on yourself. What you think of as a final judgment is more like a collaboration and a meeting when your life is complete. There is discussion—after the welcome home party and celebration, after you have had a chance to embrace those you have missed and loved, after you have had a chance to do a little rest. Then there is a review, not a judgment.

It is not a judgment, as many think, at the doorway of heaven determining that you are not allowed to return home. That is not of love! We are waiting for you; there is a review of what occurred during your life. Did you accomplish what you had hoped for? What did you learn? What do you understand? What do you wish your next steps back to the eternal light to be?

This touches on a very important issue that human beings call repentance. Repentance, as you think of it, means reparation, and part of reparation is forgiveness. It is forgiveness of those who've done you harm, and it is forgiveness of yourself both for being harmed, and for doing harm—for not acting in a way that is in accordance and alignment with the truth of who you are, which is love.

That is why you feel bad. You feel that you've lost your way, or have erred, or have either advertently or inadvertently harmed another. It feels bad because it goes against

the grain; you have injured a member of your human family, or perhaps even your divine family.

But there is not a thundering God, a punishing Father or Mother. The most severe punishment that is meted out is what you do to yourself. It is the practice of forgiveness, compassion, prudence and fortitude which eliminates the element of judgment.

So often when you lose your way, you don't want to go on. It takes fortitude and valor to continue on, to forgive yourself and say, "I will continue to try and be the love I am, to be in the alignment of my truth."

I wish to say something that may shock some of you, though I hope not: There is no difference between you and me—none. We are both born of the Mother. We are both the essence of love. We are both in service to the Mother, and in service to one another. I ask of each of you to think of me as the brother that I am, and to call on me. Call on me when you think that you have erred; call on me to share your victories; call on me to share your joys and your sorrow.

Core Issues

When I became man engaged into form, I did not carry or experience, or have the experience of dealing with hiding, removing or eliminating core issues. I was blessed in many ways because I came upon this beloved planet, birthed from the heart of my Mother, with purity, with what you can think of as a clean slate.

My sweet allies and friends, my beloved family, this is also one of the reasons why I have introduced and continued to gift you with the blessing of Karmic Dispensation. I came to know the burden of what it means to carry, deal with, challenge, clear, let go and surrender these false grids known as core issues—these emotional, mental beliefs that the human race has carried for eons.

When engaged in conversation of love with others, I often encountered a wall that would not allow my message, my being— even my love—could not climb over, or even an eye of the needle to enter through.

This initially confused me somewhat. It stymied me for I could not comprehend, either on a human or a divine level, why anyone would not wish to engage in love, for it is the most precious gift, the root fabric and element of every being.

It puzzled me why there would not be such a desire for this transformation. I retreated, reflected, observed, and listened from my perspective and from the core of my divinity as messenger for the Mother. It was difficult to engage.

I spoke truth then and even to this very day, undimmed by various lenses, filters or layers of understanding. Love, peace, joy and compassion are stand alone truths.

My quandary was why I was met with resistance when I engaged with many humans, particularly those in positions of authority, but also many who were simply fellow travelers or villagers. Why, through their lens, through their filters, this truth of love was not felt or seen or even accepted— in some cases not even examined and explored. You can imagine my dismay, and sometimes anger and concern—that I could not complete my mission, even in my mastery. I needed to discern what the blockage was.

Hence I learned, in a very clear way, this obstacle is called "core issues." Because core issues do not sit at the surface it requires a willingness—not only a spiritual willingness, but a mental, emotional, spiritual, physical, causal willingness—to engage, dig, remove, confront, and create victory over them.

This became the focus of much of my work which was in many ways lost. The messages, the energy, the spirit of love—of love yourself, love your neighbors, and act and be the love of One—has never been lost. But the translation through that wall has, in many ways, been pushed to the side.

There has been a growth of the belief in all traditions that if you pray, if you plead for divine intervention, if you meditate, if you do good works that this obstacle will be overcome. While that is a part of the solution, it is not the totality. The totality, the other piece, is the inner work of being full of valor, courage, bravery, and curiosity to discover what it is that bars you from this feeling of wholeness, of love, which is your very essence.

You may have different colored skins, different colored hair, different heights, and different weights—but there is not one being upon Gaia or anywhere that is not created from what you would think of as the super sub-atomic particles of love which comes directly from the Mother/Father/One.

You would think that curiosity would encourage you, catapult you into, not only the discovery of these core issues but into their removal so that you are free. This is a time of liberation, of quantum leaping, of jumping for the entire human race.

Why have I linked this core issue business—challenge, obstacle, opportunity—to the global conversation? Because it is through the heart-centered, honest, truthful, vulnerable, brave, courageous conversation together that allows you to see and experience the wisdom, experience and history of others which apply directly to you. You begin to see through your wisdom, knowledge and understanding that you are free to share.

This is always what I wished to promote. It was never me; it was never my beloved Mother or the Magdalena having all the answers. It was engagement, unity and connection; it was the ability to be together, to discover together, and to grow together.

Engage within your sacred self and with each other. You are glorious. The insight, pain, suffering, wisdom, and allowance you bring to the forefront are to be shared. This is the passage—this is the ascension!

The Meaning of Enlightenment & Ascension

Many of you have been diligent and courageous in your journey of spirit in form during this time of such momentous change: The unfoldment of an ascension that includes, and is reliant upon maintaining your physical form. This keeping your physical body is remarkable.

I want to speak to the magnificent brilliance of each of you; not who you will become or have been, but in this very moment how brilliant you are.

Often I hear you asking about the shift: "What will I become? How will I be different? What will I look like? What will I feel like? What will my talents and capacities be? How will I experience the fullness of my true interdimensional self?"

Let me bring you back to who you are already. It is not, and never has been about you becoming a different person. Are you transmuting, transforming, shifting, growing and increasing your frequency and vibration? Yes, in a very steadfast, consistent manner while at the same time taking quantum leaps. You have noted that in yourself; one day you feel that you are stuck in the mud, and the next day you are dancing on Venus.

The truth of this matter is about you becoming nothing other than the totality of who you really are and always have been. You are the love. You are the brilliance. You are the embodiment, interwoven with and hosting the Mother/Father/One just as you are. This is the divine perfection of whom you have always been and who you are right now.

Are you free to fly through this ascension portal? Yes, you can; you have been for a very long time. It is not merely the Company of Heaven that determines the timeline, it is also the intention, participation, action and elevation of the humans, individually and collectively. First comes the deep acceptance, surrender, admiration, honoring, respect, wonder and awe with your sacred self.

Nothing has changed, and of course everything has changed. Since the time I walked this beloved planet, my mission and purpose was the knowing and anchoring of love.

I began my mission, but did not complete it. Did I complete my time? Yes, but the mission, the shift, was not completed; it has been a work in progress all of this time.

You are the fulfillment and the completion of that portion of the mission. Is it the completion of the Mother's Plan? No. The Mother's Plan is infinite. Will you and I celebrate the completion, the anchoring, of this segment of the Plan as humanity shifts into a higher realm and state of being? Oh yes, we will, together.

There have been numerous, and culturally divergent, ways to describe enlightenment, ascension, and the fulfillment of the Divine Plan. Enlightenment is a state of being in ultimate connection with One. Is there a process of enlightenment to reach that state of being? Yes. Ascension is also a process, but ascension, in and of itself is not an outcome. Ascension is a doorway that one is passing through.

The Plan for humanity and for Gaia at this time has been ascension of the planet, the kingdoms—and most wonderfully—of humanity. It is of humanity coming to a place where they are evolved and, in some ways, returned to original pattern.

The expression "Creator Race" refers to the ability of humanity, as the holders and anchors of love in form, to have the experience of full human potential. What does that mean in practical terms?

The original core of humans was to be able to create from love. That sense, knowing and access to the divine was omnipresent, not cut off or severed. The first quantifier of experience upon Gaia within a physical form is just that, physicality. But physicality was never intended to be a prison. It was intended to be, and is in fact, a state of being where you may have the experiences of various dimensions and forms to create and experience—in delight, love, laughter, excitement and exploration—what it means to be in form. These are all expressions of love.

This latitude of being the expression in form, was for all intents and purposes, buried, misplaced and almost forgotten. There have been prophets, sages, teachers, men in the street who have raised their voices, raising the awareness throughout time saying, "Embrace, and become who you are!"

This is where the blur between enlightenment and ascension occurs. In those teachers (myself included), often the journey to that reconstitution was seen as a path of enlightenment; frequently one in which the physical body became a secondary rather than primary vehicle for experience. The body, in some ways, became disregarded. That process of enlightenment has often been viewed as an individual pathway. This journey is most often taken with the guidance, perhaps, of a sage, teacher, or guru. It is a personal path requiring diligence, discipline, great attention and longevity.

You think that ascension has been an elongated process, but from our perspective you have been flying through that portal for some time—consciously or not. I know it matters to you, beloved ones, but the level of integration has not been dependent upon your conscious awareness.

Ascension is different from enlightenment. This is a very important distinction.

The key to the expanded awareness of heart consciousness has been the anchoring of awakening—or of many steps of enlightenment in the physical body. To make it even more complex, it has been a process of anchoring this awareness in the collective; not just the psyche, or the soul, or the mental, emotional or causal bodies, but in the physical body, hence the physical realm.

What that means in practical terms is that the behaviors, actions, thoughts, emotions—the way in which your planet is constructed—shifts. It shifts from a paradigm that has been built on lack, limitation and many false beliefs into a new realm of physicality that is much broader and sometimes is termed as "enlightened."

There are many, many steps on your journey back home to the Mother. Is this ascension monumental, not only for each of you but for this universe and far beyond? Yes, it is a milestone.

You think that when you walk through the ascension portal everything changes. Do you expand, do you become the love? Yes. There is a substantial shift and change, and there is an expansion. But the point is this: Your fundamental self is still intended to be on planet to create, build and enjoy Nova Earth, and part of the Plan is to be in physicality.

This desire and implementation of a journey of enlightenment (which began long before I incarnated) is the soul memory that there is more, that incarnation is a round trip. You are birthed from the Source of the Mother/One, emanate, travel and

77

evolve—some of you for billions of years in your time, some for a brief period. It is the process by which one seeks the One, the Source, the All, the Divine, and the knowing of the Divine within. The anchoring of enlightenment, in the degrees we are talking about, is the anchoring of the divinity within.

I do not want to play a semantics game. Divinity is love.

If you are anchoring in the love, then you are anchoring in the degrees of divinity and of love. There are degrees, as it is a growth—a joining - with the All, the One, the Mother. There is always room, and for those who desire this, potential for more. Do not make the error of thinking that if you are completing your ascension, you have achieved absolute enlightenment. That is a misunderstanding.

I do not wish to minimize the impact and the expansion of ascension, because it is far greater than anything that has ever been experienced upon this planet, period. And you are well underway. The Mother declares there is no turning back; in any language you know what this means.

It is not to minimize the magnitude of what you are doing; it is beyond your expectations. I am simply saying don't delude yourself that you are becoming someone else when who you are is already perfect.

Let's assume you have gone through your ascension. Do you still, in the soul of your very being, desire further enlightenment? Yes, even more so. It is one of those paradoxes. The more you know and experience, the more you want to know and experience.

You ask, "Lord what are the landmarks, the internal events that we may look to during this expansion and ascension?" Some of you are more internally aware and more perceptually attuned to your inner workings, whereas others are more externally focused. It is neither here nor there; both are important.

Through the Tsunami of Love, the Divine Mother is multiplying Her gifts of clarity, purity and grace. You are feeling this internally in two ways, and not necessarily as step one, then step two; it is a back and forth and a balancing, until you come to the middle of your being.

What you are experiencing is further and deeper integration—a deeper solidity, appreciation and understanding—of who you really are. Within that comes clearing, because much of what you can think of as the debris and dross of core issues is being cleansed. What you are left with are the deepest illusions of separation—of recrimination, isolation, unworthiness—you may name it twelve thousand things, it will all boil down to one.

The various dressings for these core issues are frustration, irritation, disappointment or disillusion. These will come up both within yourself and it will come with others. The point is to simply observe it, participate where and how it is appropriate, then let it go, while maintaining not only your sense of humor, but your sense of balance. Balance is key.

You are part of this integration and this anchoring. You are feeling a greater sense of love, and the first definitive quality of ascension is love of self.

It is not that it is defined by the feeling, "I think I love myself more today." It is simply being awash, afloat in love so that the sense of differentiation begins to disappear. It is not to eradicate the uniqueness or splendor of who you are; the love becomes totality. You are part of that unified grid, so you feel the love for your fellow humans, for the kingdoms, the mountains, the streams, your guides and the Divine. Feeling awash in love is the key.

Think of it in terms of a washing machine; you are in the various cycles, everything is circulating at once. Externally, your perceptions and your actual experience of the external world begin to shift. If you are in that vigorous cycle of cleansing, you may well be frustrated, agitated, disappointed, etc. with the human race. But by and large, your perception and experience of the outer world—whether it is your next door neighbor, the person on the street or in Iraq—is becoming more loving, more benevolent, more understanding; it is based in passion, compassion and wisdom.

Why do I differentiate wisdom from knowing? You live in a world that is, you believe, based on facts and figures and news cycles. In our day, news cycles were news from Rome via a courier, or meeting at the well. You live in a world where you are bombarded by what you believe are facts, most of which are incorrect. Many of the facts that you need to know are either hidden or incomplete. I do not say that in a way of limitation; it is just the construct within which you are operating at the time.

As you are becoming more of your enlightened, ascended self, you are seeing through that illusion with compassion and wisdom. Wisdom is the discernment to truly be wise about what is important: what is truth, what is relevant, what contributes to your forward thrust, what contributes to the collective forward thrust, and what is in perfect alignment—not so-so, but perfect alignment—with the Mother's love.

You say, "I am looking in the external world for the signs but they are so elusive." Sweet beloved brothers and sisters, those signs are all around you; they have always been there. Are they becoming, in your wisdom vision, more apparent, more obvious because you are seeing with the heart of compassion and with your true interdimensional eyes? The answer is yes, of course.

If you are looking, be cognizant. You are an extraordinarily intelligent species. You have the innate ability to comprehend massive conceptual structures far beyond what you think of as your everyday reality.

You are looking in your outer world not

just at events but trends, waves, attitudinal shifts, heart shifts, energetic openings, transitions, transmutations. You are observing these and saying, "This is coming into graceful alignment with Universal Law."

These changes are not simply about an event, a cessation, a peace treaty or a declaration by one government. This is a wave of change that you are truly observing right now. You are observing the human trend to say that violence and gender or racial inequality, murder, mayhem, and cruelty are increasingly unacceptable.

Let me say more about why balance is the key. When you are in love—and I don't mean in the romantic sense, although that is a reflection of being the love—when you are immersed in the love, in the divine essence, then you, by definition are in balance. When you become distracted by either the internal clearing or the external drama or event of the day, then you are wavering out of the love; you are wavering, teeter-tottering out of the balance.

When you are the love, when you are embodying and anchoring the love, then you are in your place of balance. You cannot access the totality of yourself, of the interdimensional reality, of the alignment with the Mother/Father/One, if you are not in balance. How do you get to balance? We know there is much discussion about clearing and dredging, but truly the balance is maintained not just by stillpoint, but by the love.

Balance is found in the seat of your soul,

in the lower quadrant of your heart. Love emanates from this point within your heart. Once again, this is part of the blurred line between ascension and enlightenment, and it is a delightful blurred line. You move from heart loving, to being the love, to having every fiber of your being love. Your hands love, your eyelashes love, your teeth love, your hair, your skin—all your fields and particles line up, being love.

Your heart is expanding, and not only energetically. Many of you have felt the pressure of late in your heart as it expands. It is pressing outward, because it wants to encompass your entire being; it does not want that sense of delineation and differentiation. It is all of you; you cannot say, "My heart loves you, but my mind despises you." It is all of you.

I love all of you; the parts, the pieces, the aspects that you have either disdained or ignored, or aren't too sure of—or even worse, feel shame about. Let it go. I love all of you. I love all of you with all of my being, all that I have ever been, and all I ever will be. That is love, and that is balance.

When you shift interdimensionally, you are moving to a space that has always been there. It is part of the fabric, not only of this planet, but of this construct of what it means to be human. Do you experience different dimensions as brand new spaces? Yes. Think of it in this way: There is a room in your attic that has been locked for eternity; it has had all the treasures and junk locked up in there. It has been renovated, cleared, aired out, redecorated and is prepared. Unlock it and enter it!

Walk with me. Take my hand and let me show you. Let me guide you the rest of the way.

Your Integrated Self

I wish to ensure that you have welcomed in the totality of yourself, your wondrous being, your sacred self: the totality of all your aspects, all your beings, all parts, all fibers, all molecules of your magnificent, wondrous, sacred self.

We said to you that it is a time when you are calling in all aspects, all parts, all timelines of your sacred self—this is truly what you are doing. You are becoming the warehouse of you, of your totality. What you are doing is practicing unity, because your integration needs to be fully in place so there aren't fragments of you ascending; it is the unified totality of you ascending.

All timelines are basically concurrent. We know this is difficult in your reality to really comprehend this. So what you are doing in this integration work is going back to a timeline where you became fragmented, and pulling that missing piece back into your sacred self. Pull it into your conscious mind; it is not sufficient for it to be in your unconscious or a subconscious mind. See that you are beckoning, pulling and calling those aspects or fragments across the universe, and asking for those experiences, lifetimes and situations to come and anchor within you. You are doing this with all aspects of who you are—saint, sinner, martyr. Do not think of these as archetypes; you are much more than archetypes.

What you are calling in is the fullness of that experience and lifetime, of the totality of you. You do this in meditation, anchored within your heart, and you are calling throughout the universe for this experience to come in and anchor.

I don't want to make this exercise too visual because there are many of you who simply hear, feel or intuit. Feel that being that has been absent standing directly in front of you, facing you, with all their information. Prior to throwing out your arms and embracing your aspects, ask them, sweet angels, to wipe their feet. Put them through an etheric whitewash so that none of the pain, suffering, or anything that might be residual is coming through; just what is pure, clear and of love.

Then invite them in. The sensation is that they step into you, always through the portal of the heart, anchoring with you in the heart, then away you go!

Take this moment with me and feel yourself extending your arms in welcome, the same way you would welcome me, the Mother or St. Germaine. Welcome your sacred self. Embrace and bring the totality of yourself into your heart, and into every fiber of your being.

You are coming to know not simply this or that face, aspect, or mask that you have adopted during this lifetime. The biggest part of your ascension is this embrace of your totality, your divinity. Not the recognition, but the knowing of your might, power, wholeness and interdimensionality; the truth of who you are. And not only knowing it, but entering into sacred relationship with yourself.

Everything else emanates from this core relationship. If you do not love, honor, accept, surrender, cherish, and nurture your sacred self, then you are not prepared or capable of entering into relationship in the way that your heart deeply desires and demands, with others.

Long, long ago, Gabrielle once said, "All you need to return home to Source, to One, is love, trust and forgiveness, unity, connectedness and balance." If you are not in the unity, connectedness and balance of the love with yourself, then it is impossible to move forward. You will feel, time and time again, that you are hitting that proverbial brick wall.

But let me suggest to you, my beloved ones: that brick wall is an illusion erected by incomplete knowing of the psyche, subconscious and unconscious ego because it is fearful. It thinks that it is protecting you from you. Reassure it, welcome and love, nurture and nourish your magnificent self.

You are the wonder birthed from the heart of the Mother, birthed from the womb of One. In your essence, you are divine perfection. You say, "You wouldn't believe the things I've done, the mistakes I've made, the missteps." Do you really think that we don't know? Do you really think that we would ever judge you? Never. When there is a misstep we run to assist you.

Sometimes you say, "Stand back! This is a little detour I must take to learn X, Y or Z." And even if we do not wholeheartedly agree, we will step back when ordered to. But we remain in observation, vigilant; and when you allow that opening, all of us—your guides, your guardian angels, all of us who love you rush in.

That is what relationship is about. That is what love is about. It is loving you and honoring you enough to heed your desires and wishes, to help in every way we can, to love you no matter what. It is to be vigilant and wait, and to assist how, where, when, and in every way we can. It is to love you enough to be in sacred partnership with you, with each of you.

Your heart has and is exploding. You have not merely expanded; you have doubled and quadrupled, and grown at the speed of love. You ask, "Jesus, what does that mean?" It means your capacity to be the love, to engage in love, to share in love, has grown in ways that previously were simply not there. Begin this day acknowledging and loving your beloved self.

The New Male

Let us speak of the masculine experience. I speak to you as one who has been a man. I know you think of me as an ascended master, some as Son incarnate, but I have also walked as man. The beliefs and experience of the masculine stereotype—whether in the Western or the Eastern world, in the world of Judaism, Islam, Taoism or Christianity have grown out of the false paradigms of what we call the old third dimension. But even before we speak of that, let us speak for a moment about the Divine Masculine.

Our Father Creator force is love, eternal and infinite. He is the primary teacher, the moving force of the Divine Masculine behind the movement force of the Divine Feminine. Together, they teach you how to create. It is not simply strength and wisdom, although it is certainly that—infinite strength and wisdom born of infinite love. Forget the ideas of false pride, of false strength; the strength is in being genuine. Many of you have chosen to incarnate as male, as masculine, as did I; this was also for cultural reasons when I walked the earth.

Let me suggest to you, in these two-thousand-plus years, that not much has changed. There have been huge advances: technologies, society, the Industrial Age, the Information Age—and now you are in the Creator Age, reclaiming the truth of who you are, but fundamentally, not much has changed in the stereotype of what it means to be male.

The masculine, mainly because of physical prowess, has been seen—and it is an illusion—to be the leader, to be the shower of the way, not always in equal partnership with the woman. Of course, that is ridiculous beyond belief. To be the provider; to be the protector, yes. But that is because the masculine cannot in your reality be the bearer of children, or the nurturer of those children in the very beginning.

Never was gender differentiation intended to be restrictive, a hierarchy, or a way to subjugate who you are: to put a damper on emotion, a damper on dreaming, a damper on what you think is possible for you, your relationship, your family, your society or your tribe.

Brutality and aggressiveness was never part of the fiber and the structure, the essence of the masculine; we were created to be tender and caring. That is why we protect and provide—because we love and we care, and it is a way for us to demonstrate that caring.

As the old paradigms are falling away, it is glorious to see the true paradigm—the truth of the masculine emerging—and for more and more men to truly say, "I care, I hurt, I love, I cry, I embrace." This is not simply the purview of the feminine.

The pride a man takes in his accomplishments is not intended to be solely related to money or gain, control or greed. I do not say, my beloved friends, that you should not take pride in your accomplishments of work, whether it is as a carpenter, CEO, protector of the peace, physician or scientist. All of these are honorable, and it gives you a sense of accomplishment of which you deserve to be proud. But the choice of profession, of pathways—like mine—was always intended, male or female, to be in alignment with who you are: your ray, your sacred path, your sacred contract and your choices, desires and dreams.

I have been asking you to dream big, to heal deeply. This relates to how you act, not only in the outer world, but in the inner world of your worth: of the knowing of your intrinsic value, an acceptance of how you are loved and honored, and that you are love. If you strip away everything else, that is all you are. You are a particle, energy, a photon, a subatomic particle of love—and everything else is window dressing.

There is not enough celebration, even in those of you who celebrate and embrace your masculinity. You do not often enough look at yourself, at your totality, at this wondrous physical form that you have co-created with your guides and say, "Look at this, and look at what it is capable of!" Not in an ego way, but in wonder and awe that this is the unique form that you have not only chosen and designed, but that you have chosen and designed to ascend.

This isn't an inconsequential lifetime in which you simply came to experience what family life is like, or to learn lessons of humility, wealth or generosity. This is the lifetime that you have come to be in a form that is going to both carry and accompany you to a new dimension.

It is necessary to make peace with the third dimension as you transition through the ascension process. Part of this is also making peace and celebrating who you are in the third dimension as you transcend into your fifth, sixth and seventh dimensional self—enlightened, illuminated, aware, and the receptacle and giver of love. It is to embrace your physical from the perspective of the new paradigm, manifesting as the embodiment of joy in your form, in your multidimensional masculine traits.

The multidimensional men are bright agents of change—and the biggest change is the anchoring and the acceptance that they are beings of love and creators of a new reality, a new Earth. I do not suggest to you that Gaia is leaning on you to rebuild her; she is taking care of herself. The new male knows he stands in equal partnership, not with false grids and expectations, but in the full might of his ability to be, create, co-create and fully experience physicality and interdimensionality.

What does it mean to be interdimensional? For one thing, it means that you are not completely obsessed by earning money, by having towers that serve no purpose—that desecrate the air or earth or water. It means that the value of what you create and con-

tribute is what has you holding your head high.

Some of you would say to me, "I am very successful. I have money in the bank; I am admired in my community." But are you happy? Do you love yourself? Do you take time to love yourself? Do you take time to expose yourself to the wants, needs, dreams and creations of your family and community? Or do you simply keep plunging ahead?

If you are a male beggar on the street, do you feel you have somehow failed? Or do you see you are a teacher of humility, that you are a reminder for all to share the wealth, because each being has value regardless of where they sit, lie at night, or reside? This is where I want to take you. It is how I hold out my hand to you and ask you to join with me as brother. Let me help; let us begin together right now.

This old male stereotype, in many cultures—this striving, this need to prove, to achieve the success ratio, even going back to the time of being a small boy—is based on fear. I am not negating or downsizing many of your accomplishments; that is not the purpose of this conversation. But much of what you have striven for has been based on fear. "If I do not measure up, if I do not become what my father and mother want, what my grandfather was, if I do not advance the success ratio of my family, then perhaps I will not be loved."

It is a fear of not being loved, and it is the fundamental fear in your paradigm of lack of self-worth, lack of self-love; everything goes back to that. Some of you, particularly men, will say to me, "I am a sensitive guy; I know I have feelings and I love my partner and my children passionately." That is wondrous and is it not a start? Now, do you love yourself? Do you take the time to love yourself, or do you run scared every time I ask you to go deeper into your heart and embrace that love? Because no matter how deeply you think you love your children, your partner, your parents or your friends, you have not even begun to scratch the surface if you do not love yourself. Dear heart, I give you a golden guarantee—you are loved and lovable; you are the essence of love.

Sometimes it is terrifying when I say to you as men, "I want you to venture to this place that has been an abyss." My brother, I will go with you. I will hold your hand and guide you. My hand will be on your shoulder; it will be on your back. I will lead the way. I will do whatever it takes.

Do not doubt you have this capacity. It is not simply outside of you; it is within your core, and it is time right now for you to embrace this. It may be fearful at first, but once you touch it you are going to be lit up. You are going to know a sense of peace and bliss that you may never have known before, that you have only come close to when someone you know, trust and cherish has said to you, "I love you." Do not think it is just one easy step. If you falter, do not worry; I will catch you.

There will be times as you progress, that you will feel impatient that the collective has not moved quickly enough in aligning with the love. You may well feel like you have hit the wall insofar as your patience goes.

You may feel as disappointed in what is going on as I was, when I walked the streets of Jerusalem. So do not think I do not understand your position. Often, when we become impatient, when we fall down, we become vulnerable—and yes, we open our hearts and scream for help. And then we actually let it in. The answer to why the human race doesn't embrace unconditional love—as that is truly the only kind of love there is—is this wonderful element called free will. There are those that are still operating in illusion, thinking that greed and control, lack and limitation will somehow serve them.

You hit the wall because you are a teacher for others. You are one who is standing up and saying, just as I have with the money lenders, this is not acceptable; it doesn't work, stop pretending. But you also have to be the embodiment of your true masculinity, of the wisdom of discernment. So you cannot get angry. Yes, I know what it is to get angry and fed up. But when you let that go, you are also reaching out your hand to the next man who has hit the wall, and saying, "Come walk with me. Let us make different choices and creations, let us try something completely different and new."

The balancing of the masculine with the feminine within your heart, along with the acknowledgement and the embrace of the feminine self is essential. It is from that place that you are able to externalize, that you are able to embrace women in ways that are equal, meaningful and sacred. The sacred union, what some call partnership or marriage, is the balance. It is the balance in both the man and the woman of the masculine and the feminine, of divinity. It is not a contest; it is a complement.

We do not want you to eliminate ego, the same way we do not wish you to rein in or limit your mental or emotional body. Life is a question of balance. As men, we know when we are acting from ego: there is an expression, "macho," when you are strutting your stuff or insisting on being right, on being first, on leading the way—not because it is of love or truth, but simply because that is what the ego wants. When you encounter this, what I would like you to do is to embrace it the same way you would embrace a small child, because it has a great need—like a small child—to be treated tenderly and lovingly. The only reason the ego is exerting itself in such a demonstrative manner is that it is afraid of being forgotten, overlooked, overpowered. In fact, embrace and balance your ego before you start the day. Reassure it, and when it gets out of hand, laugh.

When you become annoyed with your sacred self, or become put out, angry or disappointed, what you are doing is feeding the ego. You are saying to yourself that you aren't good enough. Embrace it; laugh when it tries to flex its muscles; bring it back into the balance in your heart—and reassure it, love it, and bring it peace.

Passion for Your Job

All I have to talk about is love. My beloved brothers and sisters, within the discussion of love—is the substance, the meaning, the elements, the totality of the universe, and the totality of the Mother's heart and being.

We can talk about plumbing, gardening or my favorite subject, carpentry, and still we will be discussing love. I am on this side, but even as I walked this beloved Earth, often my friends, apostles, disciples, family, even strangers would say to me, "You only have one topic to talk about, but it is couched in many ways."

I have spoken, in other times and places, about the love and passion I have for my beloved Magdalena, for my family and children. This day I invite, encourage and support you to live, embrace, embody, and find your passion in terms of your service.

If your service is not your passion, if it is not what delights you down to your very core, then you are merely going through the motions. If you do not feel a sense of dedication, meaning, contribution, having impact,

and sheer delight for what lies ahead when you get up in the morning, then you are in the wrong job.

That's all right, because you are learning and experiencing the drudgery that others feel. It is also okay because no one is stuck. You aren't required or even asked to stay in a service that you dislike or despise. That is never in alignment with your truth, might and purpose.

If you are discontented, dissatisfied, disillusioned with the place, the work, the people or the environment that you are working in, then you are not living your passion. You say, "But I am doing my service because I am bringing light. I am acting as a transmitter and an anchor of light to these people that desperately need transformation."

What I suggest to you, my beloved friends, is that you can do that from elsewhere. You can do that in your meditation, you can do that from home or even your car. Do not put yourself in situations of service, relationship, family or anything that is less than what you deserve. If you are holding a pattern of dissatisfaction, of unhappiness, of drudgery, then you are not fully being the transmitter and the anchor. You are simply going through the motions.

You say, "But I need the money." In what universe, what reality, what dimension do you not know how capable you are of creating and earning whatever abundance you decide upon, deem necessary or desirable?

Don't you dare underestimate the truth, value, might and creativity of who you are; there is no excuse.

Create what you want. Write it in the air, write it in the water, write it on your shield and broadcast it out to the multiverse. Allow it to come to you.

When I speak about having passion for your work, I mean just that, that you are crazy about what you do! This is in every area. Are there assignments that are difficult, challenging and uncertain? Yes, because of this wonderful quality of free will that the Mother has bestowed upon Her creation. Where there is free will, there is always the opportunity and the presence of uncertainty.

I'm not merely speaking of the collective or of the human race. I am speaking of all races and all creations. Some are more evolved; some are in a place of greater alignment with divine mind, heart, purpose and will.

When I was upon the planet, there were times when my work was challenging; when blame, shame, anger, fear, fault, lack and limitation would raise their ugly heads and say to me, "You do not understand the reality of daily existence." This was not true.

There were times when it would have been far easier for me to go off quietly and practice my carpentry, to take care of my family, to be available to my Magdalena, to my mother and father. Carpentry was enjoy-able and I loved the feeling of wood—but it was not my passion because it was not in alignment with who I was, and am.

I am the carrier of compassion; the bringer of magenta. I am the teacher and the master of love, of the Christ Consciousness. Why would I want to do anything else? Even in those difficult conversations, even in those difficult assignments, I cannot fathom desiring to do something else.

I say to you, my friends, this day—find your passion. If it is not what you are doing, then adjust. If you do not know how to adjust, let me help you. I can assist in unseen and in very physical, reliable ways. As a carpenter I can help you build a new career, a new calling.

If you are exactly where your passion has led you, embrace it more deeply. Yes, it can become humdrum. Re-embrace it, recommit to it; ignite the magenta passion for who you are and for the gifts you carry on behalf of the Mother, in this unique time.

I stand and walk with you. I sit with you; I pray with you. I am in awe of you. You deserve, and have earned the right to follow your heart's desires. That is the desire and the Plan of our Mother. Express yourself in your unique way and go with my love.

Embrace Your Heart Consciousness

Love is the allowance of the grace and the energy of One: the movement of the

Mother through you, and the stillness of the Father to anchor you. It is the interconnectedness, the state of divine union and being in that place of home.

This energy descends into you. You have been penetrated more than you can ever imagine. During your entire lifetime and certainly in the last couple of years, even during difficult moments, that flow of love and of my love for each of you has never ceased.

The element I wish to speak of now is the love of your sacred self; it is the deep acceptance and embrace of your beloved being. Ascension is already underway; you can no more stop it than you can stop the movement of the universe, which is infinite and eternal. But what you can do is allow the energies to flow within you.

How do you do this? How do you allow the full impact of what is transpiring, not only on your planet but the ripple effects throughout the universe? You do it by cherishing your sacred self, by finally and fully recognizing that you are the essence of One.

There has never been a separation; there has never been lack or limitation. This is not about you rejoining; this is about you allowing and remembering the truth and the wholeness of who you have always been.

You have come from many dimensions, but all of you carry the essence of love. What this quantum leap of heart consciousness is truly about is breaking away from the

questions of, "Am I loved? Am I lovable?" to the full acceptance that you are love, and that everything—the planet, your guides, the kingdoms—carries this same essence.

You aren't leaving anything behind except a dramatic play; a story that was created by humanity in its darkest hours to control and prevent you from remembering. That is over now.

The journey we are on began a long time ago. We came very close in ancient Atlantis to succeeding with our ascension. I came in a human form as Jesus more than two-thousand years ago to remind you about love, and to replant the seeds. Now it is the time of harvest.

But let me be very clear my brothers and sisters, my beautiful family, you are not running away or getting away from anything; you are simply stepping into what is real and what has always been the truth of your being.

Is it entirely different from what you have experienced heretofore on Earth, in this lifetime, in this incarnation and in many incarnations? Yes! You are allowing the truth of your abilities and our abilities to come to the forefront so we may walk, laugh, play and journey together, so Gaia can claim and restore her true being without the impact of pollution or war, hatred or greed.

These are the things you are letting go of and, as they are literally streaming from your body and your field, you will feel lighter and lighter—perhaps a little light-headed, a little bit of displacement; that is alright. Lie down, enjoy it, and surrender.

Surrender to ascension, and love who you are. As you do this, finally you are able to love each other in fullness: without any bigotry, without illusion of what you think someone should or should not be, with the knowing there is no difference. There is diversity, there is uniqueness—but there is no separation. Every point on the grid throughout the universe is connected and it is shining brightly: know this.

During this process, allow the integration to anchor gently and softly within you. Is your world changing? Yes. But it is changing because you are changing, and it is a unique, individual experience.

Allow the changes to take place. Allow the shift to take place; do not rush it. It does not matter how long it takes; it is your time. I see your hearts and there are times where you say, "I'm not feeling too much different." That is because you have already allowed love into your being.

If any concern or fear arises, if a moment of trepidation occurs, we are on call. We are not only on call; we are standing right next to you in your living rooms, your bedrooms, your offices. The Universal Mother wraps you in Her arms. She has birthed you as She has birthed me. As you go through this rebirthing do you really think that She will not be in full attendance? Of course She is, as are Archangels Michael and Gabrielle,

Uriel and Raphael, Jophiel, Metatron, Ariel; the list is endless. Sanat Kumara watches this unfoldment and the restoration of Universal Law. There is great celebration throughout the universe.

Many times I was dismissed as crazy because I thought I could transform the world with the simplicity of love.

What I began so long ago, you my sweet angels are completing. You are the legions of light, you are the inheritors, you are the meek, you are the ones who are brave, courageous and who have stuck to your guns. They are guns of pink and they shoot flames of love, gentleness, kindness and consideration.

This is a new world and I am with you. I walk with you, stand with you. I watch over you as you lie down. Meditate and allow the shift to take place within you—because that is where it starts.

It is within your heart and being. The shift to heart consciousness is within, and then it explodes outward. You are being penetrated with light of a magnitude that you have never known or experienced, but it is meeting, matching and conjoining in union with the light that lies within you.

That is what ascension and descension are about. It is what you have offered in service to the Mother: To be the embodiment of Her promise, to be embodied in form—whether it is in the divine perfection of the body of a twenty-year-old or an eighty-year-old. That is your choice, but it will be without pain, suffering or sorrow because the illusion of separation, which is truly the root of sorrow, is gone; it is over. Do not under any conditions re-embrace the illusions of the old third dimensional realm; it has nothing to offer you and it is not where you live.

Every day, every night, we hear your prayers, your pleas for help, and your entreaties. They are all heard; they are all responded to and acted upon. It has not always been in the ways that you anticipated or that you thought you wanted. But I tell you and I promise you: your deepest heart desires, your yearning for love, as that is truly the core entreaty of every prayer, is answered.

This is not about whether ascension comes to pass or not. It is not about pass or fail; that is the old duality, and it is gone. Simply step across the portal, take the hands of your beloved ones, and come with me. We walk together in this miraculous new way. Finally I return to Earth and, my beloved ones, I am as excited as you are.

We are with you. You are love, you are loved, you are lovable, and you are co-creating this with us. We do not do this alone. We are waiting, and it is already done.

The Ascension Process

I did not come to walk alone. I did not come to be in the desert—only now and then—when I needed to struggle with my own demons and didn't wish to burden you. We do this together.

What do I mean by "this"? I wish to use the word "ascension" because it is a word, and an understanding, that we have talked about before. It is the shifting of realities; it is that interdimensional shift with the presence of your physical form.

It is the raising up of vibration, which you have already been doing. You have been penetrated by the increased frequencies for the last twenty-five years, but there has been an increase in intensity in the last year. It is in the holding of that vibration of love that you simply get lift-off.

You are assisted by many above and below, but this is not about leaving your loved ones behind. It is not about pain and sorrow; it is not about abandoning those you care about. It is about accessing and anchoring your interdimensional self. It is about traversing among and between the dimensions. I will be there waiting for you.

It is a time of transformation, and the transformation is the understanding and the anchoring of the Mother's Plan of love. It is the understanding, finally, that that is all there is.

You are seeing the breaking down, the destruction of the paradigms that have not served. When there is love, there is no room for greed or hatred, bigotry or lust. There is no room for limitation; you have never, ever been limited—you just thought you were. Let it go. Let it all go. This process of ascension is just that—a process—and it has lasted a long time. If you think that you are ready, we are more than ready. All of us join with you.

The heart decision has always been yours. I already know your heart says, "Yes."

Be in the center of your being, in the center of your beingness. It is not just to love; it is to be the love; and you are. I will walk with you again; I will sit and we will talk together again. Come with me.

Carry On

I begin by welcoming you to this time of resurrection. It is not simply my symbolic or actual resurrection we celebrate, but the resurrection of Gaia, of you, and the resurrection of Nova Being, Nova Earth, and Nova reality.

I am pleased to come to you in this time of the pause between death and resurrection, because this is the place where the formulation of the new takes place. This is the place of the infusion, fertilization and fulfilment of the dream that can explode forward into the physical reality.

There has been much said and much written about my resurrection, my return from the dead—and much written about this occurrence as a sign of my divinity. But have you ever wondered why I would choose to do that?

It has been always known that there is a cycle of life: a cycle of rebirth, the continuity of spirit in new and various forms, in and out. So what did I wish to show you? I wished to show you not only my divinity, but yours. I chose to come back—to appear—that you would know of my love and continuation in your life, whether I was in or out of form.

I remind you of your own sacred divinity, and to follow in my footsteps. It doesn't matter whether you were Jew, Hittite, Syrian, Galilean; it doesn't matter if you were Roman or Greek. Follow in my footsteps, know that you would be resurrected as well—that death is the illusion, and continuity, the everlasting life of Spirit is the truth of love.

This is especially important to understand here upon this beautiful planet of Earth. The cycles of life, particularly right now, are all around you. Gaia has taught this every year. There is a time of being in the pause: being fallow, allowing the creation of the new bud, the new shoot to take place so that the blossoming can occur again—so that the miraculous, joyful journey back to the light can occur again and again, again and again.

I won't speak about my crucifixion and death and its importance; there is enough talk of death. I want to talk about life, and the embracing of your everlasting life.

When I, the Mother, Yahweh, your guides, the Council say to you, "We know your essence; we love your essence and have known and loved it forever," we are talking of this brilliant light, this angel, this soul, that has been part of our family forever; that cannot be broken. It will not be broken—no spoke will bend, let alone break.

You are together as one, and you are together as one in life and death. We have spoken to you of the partnership of our side and yours.

Don't let your hope die; don't let your light die; hold it. When it is a fallow time, when it is a time of regeneration, when you have need to go into your cocoon, do so—and nurture the light, that it will burn brightly yet again. Simply because you are not burning like a comet across the sky, does not mean you cease to exist.

Love all portions, all cycles, and all parts of yourself—knowing that your continuity in the cycle of existence of life, and life forever hereafter, is an expression of your divinity.

When I left this planet as Jesus, most of you cried tears of bitterness and cursed your enemies in the dark; you experienced a sense of abandonment. That is why I did not wish to speak about my death this day, but rather my return—because it was the knowing that I continued on with you that was important.

I gave you everything I had. No, I don't mean my life—I mean my love, my understandings, my teachings, my time, my energy, my healing—I gave everything I had. Mary and I gave you the Thirteen Blessings and Virtues[1] long ago so that you would have the tools to continue, so that you would not feel the need to struggle, that you would not curse the darkness.

I am asking of you: to carry on my most basic of teachings—to love, cherish, honor and respect yourself as others. And in this way to create the peace that is the announcement of the new way.

If you do not cherish yourself—if you do not allow for yourself, if you do not allow for others, then you do not love others. This doesn't mean allowing your sacred self to be abused. It is about honoring yourself; it is the clarity of what is acceptable and what is not. So celebrate the resurrection of Earth, and of you.

1. "The Thirteen Blessings and Virtues" is found in The New You book.

CHAPTER 4
SACRED UNION

Sweet angels, what is the gift of sacred union? So many of you think of it in terms of partnership, and yes, of course, that is part of it. But I wish to go beyond that. It is the gift of love; it is the gift of sharing. In union is the inference and the actuality of sharing, of unification, of being together.

What is Sacred Union?

Sacred union is the gift that the Mother has given you at the very beginning of existence, when you emanated from the heart of One as that bright spark, as that light of divinity and love.

Your most sacred union is with the One, and that has never been altered, broken, or changed. It has been reinforced, not only every time you have reincarnated, but every time you have returned home. That is sacred union; it is the heart bond between Mother and you, each of you.

Within that is the deep recognition that you are of Her heart, you are of Her essence, and therefore you can never be "less than." This pervasive illusion regarding lack of self worth is simply that; it is a phantom.

I know for many it has been the monster that haunts you in the night. But I suggest to you that it is nothing more than a fleck of dust that I will blow away. I wish to do this today with you, for you, and for human-

ity, because there is no room for it; it is not of truth and it most certainly is not of love.

The second piece of sacred union is you with you, with all of you: every fiber, every molecule, every subatomic piece of you, above, below, and out into the multiverse. It is you embracing you in the knowing of your beauty, power, and indelible sweetness.

It is you loving yourself enough to say, "I am entitled and I choose my journey; I choose my creations. I will my creations, and I will Thy will because that is who I am." There is no one above, below or in between that can make you vary or stray from that truth of your whole being: your sacred union with your divine self.

You are the beloveds of my heart; you are my family and my friends. We joined in sacred union eons ago. I wish to bring this again to the forefront. What does sacred union entail, whether it is with the Mother or yourself or me? It entails service, consideration, generosity, sharing; these are all expressions of love. Turn to me as I turn to you, my brothers and sisters of Earth who are doing the ground work, who are preparing the way, and who have been doing that for a long time.

I know how hard you work–your diligence, your commitment, your stamina, your fortitude. I also want you to share with me in the joy, sweetness and unity of our hearts. This is not a gender issue, this is not a spirit/master/human issue; this is a bond of love that transcends all.

What is my gift to you? To reinforce your sacred union with yourself, in order that you may see yourself as I see you: as the bright angel, starseed, human, earthkeeper, repatterner, gatekeeper, pillar, human man or woman that you are.

I ask you this day to remember our union and bring it back to life, as it were, and then to continue on in your other sacred unions which are equally important: the union of partnership, family, friendship and community. This is not a hierarchy; these are mirrors of love.

Join Me in Joy

Walk with me and float and fly with me. Dance with me. Come play with me.

Much has been made of my time upon the Earth—how I suffered and died—and there are some who would even like to make me sound downtrodden. I don't want to be represented this way.

My purpose, my being, and my life on Earth was and is, one of love and joy. I did not spend my days worrying about what I did or did not do when I was eleven, about pulling my sister's hair or disobeying my father. Of course there were times when I disobeyed, always thinking I knew better; and sometimes I did, and sometimes I didn't.

Even as a child I loved to play. I knew the place of things in my universe, in my world; and I knew the place of play and I knew the

place of sanctity. That is why I became so outraged at the temples. Even today I repeat: The temple—the church—is not a place of commerce.

As I grew up, I took the time in every breath, in every sunbeam, in every word both to those I knew and loved, and those I only encountered in passing, to be in my center of love. When you are in the center of love, the expression is love and joy—it is gratitude; it is grace.

Joy is quiet; it is early dawn and the quiet knowing, and it is also champagne. It is all these things.

The clearing arising from the embrace of joy is dramatic. It is a conscious choice requiring the desire to move from stillness to action, back to stillness, and back to intent. It is the ever present flow of the energy. Some of you have already broken through, and are in this flow with me. Some of you are stuck, and some of you are reticent, saying, "Dear God, I have done nothing but clearing for twenty years."

Let the joy push whatever debris is in your way forward and away from you. Let your guardian angels pull it and lift it, that bubblegum, off you and out of your hair; it is simply a nuisance. Ask for the help so you may be in the totality and fullness of your being; that you may laugh and dance with fairies and elves, that you may whisper to the animals and hear their response, that you may know the Terra Gaia who is your mother Earth.

I ask you once again, will you walk with me? Not for two days out of the year; not just on Sundays, but every day; every moment.

I won't be a burden; I will lift what lies so heavily on your heart and shoulders. I will show you the golden light. I will give you my magenta heart flame. We will float on the golden river, we will fly through the portal, and we will sit in the moonlight and simply share every day.

The Sacred Nature of Partnership

I have heard many prayers asking, "Jesus, why do you not bring me my divine other, for I am lonely, and I truly desire to travel with my beloved?" Don't think those prayers aren't heard, because they are, and answered every day. You are partner with us in that creation. To enter into that partnership, into that place of sacred union—whether it is marriage or commitment or simply the decision to travel together— it is a choice. Often, I hear "Well, I didn't really have a choice." I smile at that because it underestimates their own power to create.

When I was a man on Earth, I desired to know love and relationship, to know that sweetness of sacred union. There were various opinions on this, particularly with my mother and father. We all knew the general outline of what lay ahead and the task that I had set for myself, the anchoring of love on the planet. But even as a young

man, I thought it would not make sense to be anchoring love if I did not also know the intimacy of the physical reality. I am not just talking about sexual intimacy, I am talking about joining of hearts and souls together. It is making the decision that you will travel together and that you will grow, laugh, cry and create—as individuals, but also as one.

My beloved wife, Magdalena, also knew what lay ahead. The most difficult challenges were not the politics and the persecution by the Romans and Pharisees. It was not the walk to crucifixion. The most challenging issues and moments were what we faced together as we looked at each other as mirrors: trying to grasp and understand the feelings of each other, of what the thought processes were, of what the fears were, and yes, even what the blockages were. We would do this, and it would bring us closer.

We had two children. Our first son, Samuel, died. We would have never survived such a loss if we had been isolated, but we turned to each other. In those moments of desolation and great difficulty, we remembered the joy of Mary's pregnancy and the time that we did have with our beloved son. It deepened the bond between us, and in some ways it also allowed us to know what we would face with my death, in my transition back home.

Sacred union, the commitment of heart and soul, is the greatest gift because it involves every part of you. It is ego, it is personality, it is heart, it is soul. It is putting into action what you choose to do. It is putting into action the choice to truly merge with another, as well as remain a separate individual, for it has never been the purpose of union to lose your sacred self, that unique angel that you are upon the planet. It is the greatest challenge, but also the greatest joy. It is also the greatest opportunity for growth.

I am bonded to this very day with my beloved Magdalena; nothing can ever break that bond of love. There will be lifetimes where you will join with other soul mates and soul friends, but when you make that connection it does not disappear. It travels with you throughout time and space, and when you see your beloved you recognize them; you know them by the smile in your heart and the jump in your tummy.

It is a time of differentiation; many of you are absolutely clearing the table. But do not clear it of this desire for union and partnership, because it is also a time when that dream and reality is being brought forward because you requested it. I promise you, if you turn to me, I will help you. I will help you gently, humorously and compassionately so that you may fulfill your heart's desire of knowing love in form. I am with you.

The Precious Gift of Family

I want to speak to you about the importance of family. You ask, "Jesus, how come, it is not Christmas or Easter or Father's Day?" And that, my friends, is exactly the point. Family is for every day; they are the special occasion of your heart. Family is your wisdom source, the fountain and source of compassion, laughter and tears. Family gives you the depth of understanding that will come from nowhere else in the human experience.

I have walked with you as brother, teacher, healer and friend—not as Master. I want you to understand this, for you give me many titles, but the honor I wish to hold with you is brother; brother of your heart, brother of your soul, and brother of your journey, whatever that journey entails. I know it entails a great deal and you are only at the beginning. When I come and walk with you again in the New Jerusalem I will not walk as Master; I will walk as brother and friend.

There is much controversy about my straightforward and simple love and marriage with my beloved Magdalena, the twin of my heart, twin of my very soul. How could there ever be controversy about the creation of a family, about the coming together in love? It is absurd.

My Mother and I wish to talk to you this day about my human father, Joseph. If you think of Joseph as a tree he would be a mighty oak; strong, silent and dependable. He would shield and shade you from the hard times, and he would support you; you could lean upon him.

Joseph does not get enough credit, yet there is not one father on the Earth that could do better than to emulate my beloved father, Joseph. He taught me what it was to be a man; to walk in strength, meekness and gentleness, and to have the courage of my convictions. My beloved Mother, who knew since the Annunciation what my journey would be, would often shy away and say, "Jesus, please stand back a little, do you need to be so obvious?" My father never did this. Sometimes, in the quiet of the evening, he would suggest temperance and a way of speaking that would help others understand my message. He showed me the way.

And my beloved Mary Magdalene. Do you truly think that as partners we never fought or had words? The love and passion was strong between us, but we were both very independent souls. There were moments of disagreement and moments of incredible tenderness. We did not engage on this journey together without her fully knowing of my pathway. The strength of this one was enormous, for she knew she would carry on alone, that she would be single mother.

I relied on her strength, for there were moments when I would falter. You've heard the myths, but as a human man there were times when I would simply think, "Let me take my family and run away; let me protect them and myself and let us start over." She would just look at me, and we would know not only of our sacred bond that would last

forever, but of the promise and contract that we had come to fulfill in that life—just as each of you are fulfilling a promise in this one. That is why we wish to give you all the help you can possibly get, to not limit yourself to this illusion of the third dimension. You are the Nova Beings.

Don't think in traditional terms of family. Those you find yourself being drawn together to work with, are your soul family; you are joining in a way you have agreed to long ago. You do this in support, sometimes in disagreement, but always in love. Lean on your soul family. They are your strength, your oak tree, your shade, and your sun. They are the expression of your heart. They are your mirror. Go with my love, wisdom and compassion, and go with my laughter. Lean on me.

Jesus's Family Life

More and more has come to light, thank goodness, about my life and my family. Let me begin by saying this: I loved, I adored, my family. It was arranged; because it was a culture and a time where there was adherence and understanding in a different way to prophecy and to lineage. I was born into what you can think of, in your terminology, as a privileged family. But even what you would think of today as a privileged family was not necessarily the way that we lived.

I lived in a very extended family setting. You know about my mother and father—an

102

aspect of the Mother and an aspect of Archangel Jophiel, but in human form. I wish to emphasize that my life was not sublime; it was not a human, physical journey of ecstasy. I was blessed, in the truest sense of the word, about how I came and who I was parented by, and by my grandparents. Anna, my grandmother, I loved dearly.

I had six siblings. Everybody gets confused on this issue of virgin birth, on the understanding and misunderstanding of what purity truly means and what impurity means. There could never be any question about the purity of my mother.

Following my birth, there were many children. That was powerful and right, because from a very early age, I was not always singled out as the special one. I had to learn to behave, to adhere to what you would think of as family structure, strictures, behaviors and customs.

There was a great deal of study for me; there always was in families of our nature. Did I receive a lot of instruction? I did, particularly from the rabbis. My schooling was not simply restricted to Judaism; it was very broad. Joseph taught me how to be a young man, and then a man. It was Joseph, my father, who taught me patience and silence.

My nature, particularly as a child, an adolescent and a young man, was that I always wanted to tell everyone what I perceived, what I already knew. Joseph taught me the importance of balance. I could not have healed, could not have taught, could

not have stayed the path if I had not used, learned, remembered and embodied the Divine Qualities my parents taught me, and my siblings reinforced.

Who you think of as Mary Magdalene, the Magdalena, was my beloved wife and in so many ways my other half, my sacred other. The Bible contains many stories of my life, but it has been severely edited, particularly those stories.

There were two streams of thought: One wanted to simply maintain power and exclude women. Another wanted to keep me in the divine realm and not to show me as a man, prophet, and teacher as well.

It would have been significantly contrary to custom for me not to marry. I was completely, madly in love with my Magdalena. From the very first moment I saw her, we both knew. We knew of our mission and purpose together, and we knew the path that lay ahead. That did not stop us from having our life together in great joy, passion and love. We were fulfilling and modeling sacred partnership.

The Magdalena had her own training which was also extensive, particularly with the Essenes. She was the one who brought ritual; she was a channel long before she met me. She continued to channel and to perform ritual and sacred ceremony; that is what she brought to our partnership.

What she also brought was joy, and the creation of family. We had two children.

First, a little boy, Samuel Thomas James, sometimes called David. We had many names in those days; everybody needed to be included and honored. Our son died when he was three. He was the brightest light; he was the gift that we had been given. In many ways he was our hope and the continuity, because we also knew that my life would not be long.

We had a daughter, very much like her mother. Our beloved Sarah became our lineage, our vessel, our hope: bright and beautiful. When we knew that my time was coming to conclusion, my Mary wanted, in many ways, to simply come with me. It is often this way, when you are truly in sacred partnership. You even see it now; people will die close to one another.

But our promise was that she would live to teach, protect, and bring Sarah forward. That is why, even though there were many political reasons and those who would like to have wiped all of us out—the Magdalena was brought to a place of safety. What we began in love continued on, and still does to this day.

I bring you my blessing of love this day, as you begin anew, as each of you is reborn into your totality. I am at the portal waiting. Come join me.

Why Should Love Wait?

On this planet, in the universe, through-out the creation of the Mother/Father/One, there is truly only one drive. Oh, there is a drive to maintain human life, to eat, to sleep, but that is not what I am talking about. The one drive is to love.

The yearning is to experience love; to give and receive love; to know you are loved and lovable, but that you are the essence of love. You are at a point, my sweet family, where that knowing is upon you.

One of the things that is occurring in that growth, expansion and ascension, is the yearning for love has become persistent, consistent, undeniable. It is a driving force, and to this I say, "Hallelujah!" Because what was my life about other than teaching love? I was trying to awaken humanity to the truth of love; to cherish one another and themselves so they could be healed, so they could expand, so that they could change the world.

That message and drive has never died. In fact, it has never been stronger and more evident upon this planet than right now. The tsunami of love the Divine Mother is washing you with day, night, and in-between is preparing you for sacred union. In many ways it is the baptism before the marriage; it is the cleansing before the full union. You are ready to fulfill your desire to unite. As one who has walked fully as man, as human, I can assure you: you are prepared to love yourself.

The Mother's love is washing you, inside and out, cleansing you, integrating and anchoring within you. Aside from washing away the horrific debris, what is the end result of the Mother's tsunami? It is that you are now fully prepared. You are in a state of grace to enter into union with yourself; to love, cherish, honor, admire and commit; to fulfill your dreams, your mission and purpose, your desired creations. Not next year, not next month—but right now. You are prepared to enter into union with your twin flame, your circle, this Council of Love, and with the entire human race.

Are some still being washed by the tsunami? Yes. And it is intensifying, so get ready! You are taking it to the next step, the next level. I am there with you, with my arms wide open, as is my beloved Magdalena. It is time, not only for sacred union with yourself but reunion with us. I refer to today, tomorrow, and the weeks to come. Let us begin.

Why should love have to wait any longer? Why would you choose to wait any longer? Your design, your heart, your grid, Earth's grid is in harmony and alignment. What is the next step after alignment? It is what I speak of: sacred union.

No more excuses, no more false grids. Embrace your perfection in what you have so often judged as your imperfection. Let us grace each other and join our hearts as One.

Love Is Contagious

When you are in sacred union with your beloved self, the sense of urgency to focus on bringing in cosmic and divine love dissipates, and the desire to radiate out that love to the human collective grows. It is a bonus of sacred partnership that begins with sacred partnership with yourself, which grows and is amplified.

Why does this happen? Because when you have anchored the love of self, you are prepared and ready to engage in sacred union and partnership with another. It is one thing to finally and deeply commit, know and love yourself, but as I have said, this is the starting point.

When you join with your sacred partner, it is not just an addition or multiplication of two. In our reality, we tend to deal more with squaring than multiplication. What happens is a squaring of the your energies, because the realization that comes in the acknowledgement and union of sacred partnership is that you are indeed cosmic love and divine essence. You are loved not only for your divine essence but for who you are right now. Not merely for your large, integrated self, but for the person that you are right now at this point in your ascension process, in your journey back to the One. This is because you have deemed and discerned, not judged, yourself to be magnificent. It is a bubbling up that is bigger than Mount Vesuvius! And it can't and shouldn't be controlled; nor do we guide you to do so. Love is infectious; it is absolutely infectious.

What changes (and I speak from personal experience) is that you no longer feel like you are constantly going to the well to fill up and then beam out; fill up and then do your sacred work. You finally get it: your well is full, and it's inside you. That hesitancy, that pause that I have often spoken of, is eliminated. You are the constant flow; you are the conduit of personal love, of divine love, of true healing. This is what the Mother is talking about when She asks everyone to fall in love with each other. When that is happening—and it is happening, sweet angels—it changes the world.

When you are in love with everybody, because it is contagious, you cannot wreak havoc on one another; you cannot go to war against one another. Inside love; inside this wonderful, bubbling pot on the stove is peace, joy and clarity. That is the shift that so many of you are feeling. That "going to the well, coming back, going to the well, coming back, fill me up so I can transmit" is shifting. You are realizing that you are the well. And not only that; is it not the most remarkable amount of fun that you have ever had?

In these relationships, the sacred unions that are being formed are of a high vibration that has never existed at this level before. This is one of your markers for ascension: you are capable and you are engaging in sacred partnerships that are of a much

higher vibratory frequency and in a higher octave than before.

The love is there, it is percolating, boiling on the stove. That love that is boiling on the stove does affect what you think of as the challenges, such as money or geographic distance.

You ask, "Lord, how can that be?" Let me give you a visual sign. The love is boiling on the stove and the vapors are rising. It is a never-ending filled pot, so it is not going to go dry. The steam is rising; it is moving out into the universe and it is addressing (in ways that you do not know because you do not fully understand, as yet, how sheer energy works) the variety of what you think are difficulties. Simultaneously, you are addressing those issues of what you think of as the bigger picture. So, dearheart, do not be distracted; keep the pot boiling.

Receive the waves of the Mother's tsunami of love. Never judge what another person's reticence or their perceived obstacles are. Allow the love to come to you; the Mother's love, that tsunami, to penetrate your screen and remove resistance. Let it flow freely right through you; it is an independent process that clears you to enter more clearly and fully into that sacred partnership that you are desiring.

Allow me to share with you a visualization of opening to the Mother's tsunami of love. See that the trickle has started, the river is gaining force; see that you are holding hands with those you love. The circle is seven billion people wide and it encircles the Earth; it is one circle. You are all holding each other up, and we are holding you up as well. We are not behind you, we are in between you, so that you can lean on us, so that the currents of the Mother's tsunami move right through you, swiftly, fully, pervasively, and completely.

Where there has been injury, embrace forgiveness: forgiveness of the injurer and forgiveness of your sweet self. Forgive that there has been hurt, pain, hostility, bitterness. In the forgiveness is the letting go. I forgive you. I release you to your path as I release me to mine. Make sure, dearheart, that you also do the meditation for Karmic Dispensation, so there are no cords at all.

Where there is fear, ask your sweet self what are you afraid of? You are afraid of not being loved; you are afraid of not being seen for the bright totality of who you are. You are afraid of being overlooked, overrun, controlled and of not being nourished the way every child and adult desires to be.

Invite that aspect of the fearful, lonely child in through the portal of your heart, and offer love and comfort. Eventually you will have the empathy, the compassion for the person who does not see, perhaps, as clearly as you desire. Then, touch their heart; do the laser beam with your index and middle fingers to their heart. Eventually move into the gift of the infinity sign between the two of you. This will eradicate what has plagued you all these years.

When you do these things, you are bringing back the sense of unity, love, connectedness that you know from this side. You are bringing back old friends mostly, that you have traveled with forever and that you have agreed to go to the masked ball with, to dance together, and be together at midnight when you unveil who you both truly are. What you are bringing back to Earth is the renewal and the revelation that you are already in connectedness and love. It is the remembering—it is remembering love.

Anchor yourself in the love. Not in the old third dimension, because that is of judgment, fault, blame, shame, guilt; there is no place for that. The ego is not to be banished, but to be embraced; it is a delightful part of who you are. We have no desire to eliminate the ego or the personality; it is just to be in the balance of the truth.

What you are often fearful of is someone putting something over on you; that you are not being vigilant enough to make sure that everybody is doing what they are say they are doing. There is a difference between being vigilant and being judgmental.

It is only fear that leads to judgment. It is fear that what you do (how you see, behave, act and interact, supervise, work—the list is endless) is not good enough. The fear is of loss; loss of face, employment, or money. But that is not the truth of who you are. I would have this difficulty sometimes, you know, with my apostles or disciples. They would say, "That person listened and their heart was open, and then they went home and they beat their wife. We should exclude them; they are not following your law, Lord."

I would say, "Don't be ridiculous. Let us go to that house, one of you. Let us take that brother aside and speak to his heart and find out what the fear is: what is that demon that is lurking inside and making him feel that he must choose violence over love? Let us coach him, let us support him, let us speak to his wife, and let us discuss strategies that will help."

The truth of yearning for love, the yearning for sacred partnership is embedded within your core, sweet angels. Do not ignore this truth. Use these tools I offer you. And then choose love. Why? Because you deserve it, it is your birthright.

Every day, when you are going to the office, anchor yourself in the 13th Octave, in the heart of God, in the heart of Mother/Father/One. Then proceed with your day.

When you see a situation where you think you are reactive and being judgmental, put up the red flag and stop cold in your tracks. Say to yourself, "That is not of love, which is not of who I am. Let me see the truth of this situation—not through the eyes of lack, not through the eyes of fear—rather, through the eyes of love. What does this situation really need in order to zoom forward and be corrected?"

Spend no time thinking about being afraid of this or doing it wrong. Just move directly into course correction, which makes everybody feel good.

Go with my love, always and forever.

The Dynamics of Family

I welcome all of you who I call my family. You ask, "Jesus, how could you have such a large family? How could you possibly hold such love for so many within your being, within your core, within your heart?" I carry the infinite ability of the Creator/Source/One, and so do you, my beloved friends.

Your ability to love transcends everything. It is the fiber of your being, the core of your essence, the air that you breathe, the light that you see, and the reason you are alive. You came in service to the Mother/Father/One, particularly to the Mother. You came during this time of transition and ascension to complete what we began so long ago, and to begin anew. This is not the end; it is the beginning. It is the beginning of what has always been planned. It is not simply the fulfillment of the Mother's Plan; it is the fulfillment of your plan.

Many of you have walked with me. The discussions we had so long ago when we walked the hills and the streets of Jerusalem and along the Sea of Galilee haven't changed. For even then you would ask, "Jesus, how could I be born into this family?

They do not understand me; they do not understand my rebelliousness against the traditional ways. They do not understand why I walk with a barefoot prophet. They do not understand what it is that you are trying to accomplish by challenging the rabbis and Romans."

Then you would ask, "And what of my wife? She expects me to support her and our children. I know that I must take care of my family, and yet here I am walking with you instead of fishing or doing my trade. I cannot even explain myself, Lord. How do I explain this to my family and to those I love? Yes, we have differences of views but they are of my house, of my lineage, and I not only love them; I honor and respect them, even though I do not agree with them. So, how do I proceed?"

I said to you then and I say to you now: Proceed bravely; not ruthlessly, not without consideration, and never in judgment. But do what you must, because your heart and soul demand it. If on some days that means baking bricks, then do so. If it means going fishing to feed your family, of course you must do so. But if your soul demands that you walk, meditate, pray and connect, then do so.

I was fortunate, because I knew and understood the family I was being born into, and who was claiming me. I was privileged in so many ways. I was blessed later with a wife and children who also understood me. This did not mean that there were not moments of disagreement, chaos, or misunderstanding; there were.

There was always extended family with us, close by, for that is how we lived. Very often there were varying opinions, and there were always opinions about what I was up to. Even my beloved mother—who knew my path, my journey, my mission—would sometimes hesitate and ask, "Can't you stay home today? Can't you adhere to convention, to the law? Can't you be less conspicuous?" There was sometimes debate and sometimes dissension, because they felt I was willful and not honoring my mother. But, of course, I was truly honoring my Mother and Father, and that was beyond debate.

I understand the dynamics of family. I understand the joy, peace, and support of family. I also understand disharmony, conflict and confrontation, as well as what it means to go in a direction that is not understood or agreed to. I understand why you have chosen the family that you have incarnated into, in this configuration; it is to learn, but also to teach.

There is a time to stretch your wings and fly. That is particularly true when you have practiced love and acceptance, and have shared freely with your family who you are and what you are up to.

I speak to each of you who are fearful of speaking to their families or exposing themselves about who they are and what they believe; they are so afraid, not just of judgment, but also of not being loved. This reflects the fact that the belief, not necessarily the reality, but the belief is that they are not loved unconditionally. Therefore, they have not had the experience, the feeling, that they are fully loved. It feels conditional upon maintaining some level of persona that may or may not be in keeping with who they really are.

I encourage each of you to be honest—not in a confrontational way, as that accomplishes nothing, but to simply be forthright and honest about who you are, what you believe in, and what you are trying to accomplish with your life. You do not even have to say that you are working for the entire planet and the Divine Mother, but just for your own life.

If you have done that and feel that you are only becoming battered and bruised, then you have to say, "I will love you from a distance, and I will give you room to grow, to follow your journey and path of awakening, enlightenment and spiritual growth; so that you will reach a place—receiving my love and support from a distance—where you can see who I am, where you can begin to engage in love for me as who I am."

There is also a time to leave that nest when it is so comfortable and comforting. I'm not saying that you cannot return, but your work, your mission and purpose is not just to find that place of love and harmony with your family; it is to find it within yourself and to take that out into the world

and share it with people. Those people may begin as strangers but will become your friends, your circle and your soul family.

For those of you wondering if it is important to reconcile with family members prior to ascension, it depends on your circumstances. For some, that reconciliation is done completely etherically—in meditation, on a soul level. For many of you it entails forgiveness. Surrender the idea of what you thought or felt or hoped your family dynamic might be. Reach that place where you can send love regardless of the conditions.

For some it is done in person or via electronic media that is so readily available these days. It does not need to be involved; in fact, in most situations, it is simply saying, "I love you." Whether you have argued, been estranged, had severe differences of opinion or been on the same track, it is simply saying, "I love and honor you, and I thank you for what you have given me, what you have shown me, what you have taught me about myself, and how you have contributed to the fulfillment of my journey."

For some, it is not possible to reconcile in person. But it is always possible to do in meditation and soul conversation, calling the person's higher self forward and addressing them in a loving and mutually honoring way.

This is one of the fundamental ways in which you make peace with the third dimension, because the family as you have known it, in all its permutations in the third, is something that changes rather dramatically as you enter a higher realm of understanding, of heart consciousness and of awareness. I am not saying that the family disappears. It doesn't. But the awareness and the connections, and what you think of as family changes radically.

Many of you have gone through multiple marriages or relationships of an intimate nature, and there has been some incomplete resolution, some blame, fault and guilt. What you need to reconcile is that you went through those relationships because each of them contributed not only to you, but to your partner. You were learning something, you were growing. Now, it is time to make peace with them, to embrace them, to thank them, and to send them love.

If you are feeling disenfranchised or disconnected from your biological family, please know that your families of origin and the family you have assumed along the way have gifted you in seen and unseen ways. For example, they have made you more aware of your desire to be with your true family of origin—your soul family and soul circle. It has catapulted you, acted as a catalyst, for you to seek out who you are truly, creatively, in harmony with. There is enough love for everybody. You tend to think of this in terms of fragmentation, in terms of having to choose either/or and it is not that. There is enough love to go around. Don't ever think you need to choose

between either or.

Many of you have thought of divorce as tragedy, and yet the extended family is what the Mother has created in order to teach you. Those children have four, or six parents—and that is a good thing. When approached with love and sensitivity, there is an understanding that the more children are loved, the more creative, freer, and expansive they are.

As you look at the one that you have perhaps had the most conflict, abuse, confrontation, or disagreement with, you may see it is simply that they have lost their way. Looking at the circle that you have incarnated with again and again, you may see how deeply they love you, and why they incarnated with you.

You do not tend to incarnate with those who are very distant in terms of family. Does it happen? Yes. Is it typical? No. When you are on our side and you are deciding to go, especially with such an important mission as this lifetime, you have turned to those who are closest to you and said, "Alright, now this is what we want to achieve." And because the bonds and the love are so strong, you come together. Now has that gotten waylaid? In many cases it has. That is the gift, and the trauma, of free will. Go back to the original agreement about why you came together; it was because you loved and trusted each other so deeply.

At the end, when you relinquish your form and reunite with everybody you have known, you may well shake your head, laugh and say, "Oh, that's what that was about."

Go with my love, and love your family, whoever they are. Go in peace, dear ones.

Why Did You Choose Your Family?

It is time for you to expand how you think of your precious self whom you primarily define by what you know and cherish: your physical, mental, emotional and spiritual makeup. Expand that knowing into your angelic, earthkeeper, interdimensional self. Expand this understanding, cognizance, recognition and acceptance, not because you are in any way lacking or insufficient, but because you are magnificent.

When I walked on Earth I brought my divinity and my multidimensional understanding with me. But it didn't cancel out, or in any way diminish or eliminate my experience as three-dimensional person. What I am asking of you is to see and acknowledge the massive nature of your being.

I talk about the importance of family. Within that I include your biological family who you know in this lifetime, your angelic family, your Earth family, your family of humanity, and your soul family—some of which are on Earth, and some who are with us on this side—and in the far reaches of the multiverse.

Lack of visible presence does not make someone less a member of your family. If you have a cousin living in South America, and you live in Northern Canada, it does not diminish or eliminate the fact that you are cousins. In fact, it may be the closest familial relationship you have. I am not simply speaking of physical proximity, but let us begin this discussion with the understanding of those relationships of physical proximity.

In this, I am not so much addressing those of you fortunate enough to have kind, loving, supportive and accepting families. Yet, know that to achieve that place of support within families is not always easy. I do not presume or wish to give the impression there have never been bumps along the road in these supportive relationships—of course, there have been. There has been a lot of effort put forth to form what you think of as happy families.

There are many of you, my beloved friends, who look around you and think, "Why am I in this family? What was the idea or plan? Why am I not seen, loved and cherished for the very truth of who I am? Why, when I push and try to form relationships, does it cause conflict, or worse, simply dismissal and being ignored?"

Let' start with the simplest explanation which I have repeated thousands of times. You came to teach love. That is the short answer, and with all the window dressings, accoutrements and fine tunings, that is the long answer. You came into that family to be the beacon and carrier of love; it is that simple. You came into that configuration—whether they were absolute strangers or beings that you had traveled with time after time—because there was an opening and an agreement.

You did not do this blindly, or in a foolhardy way. There was an opening and an agreement—that those who were part of your family were ready to experience, give and discover love—and in the purity of your being, in the sweetness of your soul, in your compassion, you said, "Yes."

It was never a mistake or a misstep. That mission has never changed. For some of you, that opportunity to teach love is still open, particularly as humans grow, change, evolve and prepare for the choice of ascension. But for others of you, either for reasons of survival, self-protection, or continuity of your being and your path—which is ultimately your responsibility—you have stepped away from that mission of being the anchor of love in your family. There is no right or wrong.

Yes, you were born into your family of origin with a very specific mission, purpose and design. It was not simply to open their hearts, but also to help you flourish and grow; to support you in your journey of becoming.

You all came—even those who are naysayers—with the absolute knowing and understanding that this was a time of phenomenal massive change. There was no one who

came during this time of ascension/transition/shift that was not fully equipped and aware.

The combinations of families of origin were not only to bring love, but also the supports that were necessary to catalyze you on your journey. No one came and said, "I will be put in a family that is abusive and brutal, and this will help me on my journey." That was never part of your plan or the Divine Plan; these are human free will choices. This is the plan gone awry at the worst level.

Let me be clear about this, brutality, abuse, hatred, greed and meanness within the family are the most egregious acts of all. It is personal; it is directed; it is cruel. You may compensate and say, "That brutality, or abuse, or just being ignored, or not being seen made me stronger." What you did, dear heart, was make the best of a bad situation. But we would never suggest to you that this was the idea or plan of what you would bring forth on this planet.

Do you need to make peace with it? Yes. For some of you that means leaving them behind, for some it means leaving the door slightly ajar, for others it means building bridges. But those are your decisions, and those decisions are based on two factors: What is of love, and what assists you and the collective in moving forward on your journey of ascension?

The guidance the Magdalena and I, as a family, offer you is this: If you have lost, or have not been fulfilled in your family

"The time is now. I am in your midst. You can see my face."

of origin—do not give up. For those of you who have been fulfilled in your family of origin, the advice is exactly the same. Keep going, because now is a time upon the planet where it is important to expand and embrace the idea of what family is—the concrete reality of what is family.

We often speak of soul family; these are the beings that you encounter through meditation on this side; and in human form with whom you have such a rich, beloved bond. It is not simply a bond of saying, "Oh, I think we are connected." It is a bond, in this time and energy of transition that catalyzes action together. Sometimes the action is simply the sharing of heart—of experiencing, knowing and acknowledging love. Sometimes it is coming together to create and undertake magnificent projects which will be the future of Nova Earth.

Your soul family is more important than ever. Many of you yearn for your soul family and friends: to sit, walk, talk and be together. It is a straightforward heart yearning. Think of it in this way - you meet someone and you have the immediate deep knowing: "I know this person; I like this person. I think I love this person and we can be the best of friends." After the initial meeting—after you have sat together and talked each other's ears off for hours—there is this yearning: "When can we get together again? What do you want to do, what do you want to explore, what do you enjoy doing? Let's do it together." When that

yearning is not reciprocated you are disappointed. But when it is, the chemistry, love and union are deep gifts.

With soul family there is a greater interconnectedness of mind, while honoring the uniqueness and individuality. There is a complete group unity consciousness. Yet the preciousness—the gift of individuality, of uniqueness of your spark of love being different, from mine or from someone else is treasured.

Is there shared biology? More than biology, there are shared energetic grids. Think of it as your template, your beautiful unique snowflake soul design. Your template is your point of reference and connection with many outside of your biological family. For many of you, your strongest terms of reference are with that soul family that is angelic or elemental, rather than human being. It is a matter of, "To whom do you relate most closely? For whom do you yearn most deeply?"

Many of you feel that you have known me as a friend or family member when I walked the Earth. You wonder if those memories and feelings are accurate, or whether there is a collective memory, or are we soul family. My beloveds, it is both. There are many of you I have known and touched and laughed and broken bread with and that I have always thought of as part of my family. It doesn't matter whether it was a distant cousin, or one who stood on a hillside as a deaf child waiting to be healed.

So, yes, many of you have known me; and many of you know me as part of your soul family. The world was quite literally a smaller place then, so many of us have agreed to reunite in this way. It is much the same in different traditions and in different religions, and I do not mean the dogma, but simply the practice of spirituality. They are re-encountering their beloved masters as well.

But is there a connection in the human DNA that we share? I do not exclude myself, nor would St. Germaine or Lord Maitreya or the Buddha; the answer is yes. We do share that memory which is literally part of the DNA. It was part of the promise so you would not forget. You said, "I will go and have many of the memories veiled, but I need to know of this very important connection. I need to know that your support and love is there." So it is embedded in you, the same way it has been embedded in me.

Unsupportive Families

We have spoken a great deal about intimacy and particularly about the partnership aspect of Sacred Union. Is there more to be said? There is always more to be said, but I wish to speak to you about the expansion of this sacred relationship and how one engages with family.

I had the most magnificent parents when I walked the Earth as Jesus; it does not get any better than my Mother Mary and Joseph. For that matter, it doesn't get any better than my brothers and sisters, whom I adored.

So often, people say to me, "You had it really good. My family is a horror show." I hear you when you say that, and I also hear the yearning of your heart to have deep, meaningful and loving relationships with your parents, siblings and family.

Why do I bring this subject up? I had a very large family; in the days when I walked the Earth, the extended family was the norm. I had many aunts, uncles, nephews and nieces, and then there were those—you still have this custom today—where, because someone is part of the community, they become the honorary aunt or uncle.

Because I walked a different path, all my family had opinions—and they weren't always supportive. Some were enormously supportive, giving me the courage to carry on, reminding me of the sacred nature of family. But you all know there is a difference between being reminded that family is important and being badgered to pay attention to your family.

There were many who would say to me, "Jesus, what do you think you are doing? You are causing such pain, upheaval and humiliation for the entire family. Your poor mother! Your poor father! Your poor wife! When are you going to get some sense into you? Come with me back to the synagogue. Let us pray together and hope that you will be guided to sanity."

Well, what was I to do? Often I would say, "Thank you. Thank you for caring enough about me to express your opinion and belief. Thank you for loving me and my immediate family enough to take the chance of stepping forward, in what may seem to be an offensive or an aggressive manner, because you care so much. I believe I am on the right track. I am guided by my Father above and my Mother below. Do not be overly concerned about me."

Sometimes, when it was a particular uncle that I really loved, I would say, "Let's go to the synagogue and pray, Uncle Josh, because, let's face it, you could use some further guidance!" We would laugh, hug, and go and pray. So there was a mixture of allowance, of love, and of what they most certainly viewed as defiant behavior, but also a consistency in how I shared my truth. I did not stop love, loving and cherishing my extended family because they didn't agree with me.

Did I try to avoid them? Yes, I must admit that! There were many times where I would say to Mary, "Let's just duck out the back. I'm not in the mood for this conversation." But there were many occasions when I could not avoid it. Did I betray, or try and adjust, or tone down who I was? No! Did I use humor, did I use compassion, and did I feign deafness? Yes!

I say this because all of you, my beloved family, have those in your life who think they are simply shining a light for you, and bringing to your attention that you are dead wrong! That is because they care, or they are just committed to the fact that they are always right.

Bless them, cherish them, and send them on their way—they are being touched, prodded, opened and cleansed by the Mother's tsunami of love. Stand back, be the observer, share what they can hear with their hearts—and let the rest alone.

Change is underway, and you can be the observer and see the miraculous shifts in them right before your very eyes. You are far luckier than I was in that lifetime. So many of them stood back, even at the crucifixion, and said, "See, I told you no good would come of this."

Be patient, but be vigilant. Be true to who you are. Love them unconditionally—but obedience is not a requirement.

Your Team Is With You

Trust is usually in the bailiwick of our beloved Mother, Universal Mother Mary, the one that walked the Earth to tend to me, as infant, as child and as man. How I trusted her, my guardian angel on Earth.

Often, she and I would have different perspectives, different agendas, and different ways of approaching the world. What you don't know is that I could be a fairly impetuous young man and a terrible teenager. I would simply go and do what I felt my Father told me to do. Well, there were times when it literally made my Mother and my beloved Earth father Joseph, pull out their hair. And then we would sit and we would talk, and I would trust their guidance, because I knew it came from a place of love.

You also feel the need for similar support, for that love and trust, not only of above, but below. When you have incarnated, you have brought your team with you. Just as I had my family, my disciples, and my apostles—so my friends, do you. But sometimes you just don't know it. I speak of this because when you are asked to step forward, as beings of light and truth and love, you need to have this circle of love. You have need to have with you like-minded beings, human beings, who share your thoughts, dreams, ideas and who support you as you go forward.

Look around you and see—you are surrounded by your team who know, love, honor and cherish you. This was arranged long before you incarnated. It is the support and delight of being in form as a vessel and messenger of love. Accept and embrace those who surround you. Know and love your team. Thank them for their being in your life, and acknowledge their role in your unfoldment within the Mother's plan.

Look for Me Everywhere

I have walked this Earth many times, as companion, prophet and spirit. I walk it again as your brother and friend. But I also come to teach. Your world and your universe have changed and there is celebration throughout the heavens. There is need for a realization of this wondrous fact of miracle within your hearts.

You have been gifted with the ring of Archangel Gabrielle, the diamond of brilliance and clarity. It has been transposed into your cellular structure, so that you will shine as the brilliant beings you are. These diamonds are transmitters of the energy of love. Trust in your sweet self, in your own heart and island within. Don't shy away from your brilliance, from your beauty or from your full potential.

You don't walk alone. You walk in twos, and threes and legions. You are units of one, but never alone. Allow that aloneness to slip from you, and walk even in the most silent, private moment in union and partnership with your divine self.

You are cleared and ready to come to this feast that has been prepared. It is a feast of love. Open your hearts, larger than your beings, larger than any building, state or planet. You are my emissaries and friends. That is why I have gathered you. Not from religions, classes or structures, but from everywhere. Because the message of love and the light of being has need to be felt everywhere. Turn to your fellow beings and see yourselves in their eyes. Turn to me and see me in them.

Shed your issues of self-worth this day and celebrate victory. As I have healed many, in many lives, now you have been gifted with the tool to heal all: yourselves, each other, and this planet. Do so in the name of love, and do so in the name of your sacred selves.

Remember the times we have spent together in all forms and ways. It is time to bring those lifetimes forward to conscious remembering, not because you are this or that person, but because you have knowledge, understandings, love and strength that you have blocked. Those blockages are gone. So remember: In India, in Galilee, in China, the times we spent together; and in the remembering, know that we will spend time again on this green planet of Earth.

Welcome me as your brother into your hearts and homes, into your families and community, for it is where I will belong; beyond denomination or culture, simply in love, in acceptance. I come to serve and I will have my trials and tribulations and I will turn to you as you have turned to me and we will have our victories. In this way, we have life. Look for me everywhere for I am with you.

Engaging Community

Welcome, brothers and sisters to this time of union, to this time of love in twos and threes and thousands. You no longer need to walk alone; your time of solitary confinement is over. If you say to me, "But Jesus, I walk alone and I do so joyfully," I will tell you that within your sacred self, there are thousands of aspects, so no one really walks alone.

It is a time of reaching out, of cementing your relationships on this planet with each other. In this way you cement relationships with your brothers and sisters throughout the universe, above and below.

I have great faith in you, and my patience is infinite. It is time for you to know the joy of union, fully and completely, with one another. I am not speaking only of marriage partners or sacred partnerships. Friendships and family are also essential. But so is the partnering with your communities and with each other essential, for it is not enough to say, "I have joined with another and we are in the bliss of marriage." This is only part of what you have chosen; there is still a huge segment of you left to share.

Yes, there is always more to go around. There is no limit to love. There is no limit to what you can accomplish, but it must begin within. I do not seek to change you, for you are solely perfection. What I seek to ask of you is to open your hearts yet further, and to allow this perfection to shine unto each other—in action on earth.

Do not sit in the closet and pray; join me in the streets feeding the hungry, tending the wounded. That is where we belong, in partnership with our brothers and sisters in compassion. You are teachers; you are my

120

partners in changing this planet.

Notice, I will walk with you—but first you must choose to walk with me. Hear me, and join me in heart. Come laugh and play because it's time for resurrection for all of us.

Difficult People

There are times, beloved angels, when you will encounter those individuals, groups and situations that are difficult and exceptionally challenging. That does not mean that you don't proceed and engage. But there are specific ways in which it is best, most fruitful, to proceed to open their hearts and minds to sacred union.

First and foremost, the best method is two fingers to the heart to open, unlock and remove their resistance. But before that, let us talk about what you call difficult people. When I walked as Jesus, I had my share of difficult people. You, whether you are living in a terrible war zone or in a very pleasant situation, all have difficult people.

I do not wish to speak in euphemisms so I will not say to you, "These are your opportunities," because is it not frustrating when people speak that way while you are pulling out your hair and saying, "I don't really need this opportunity at this moment?"

But in fact, it is exactly what you have created and called forth, or that they have created and called forth, because difficulty is always, minimally, a two-sided affair. These are some of your greatest teachers; the difficult people remind you of what has not been addressed, what has not been resolved, and what remains to be done—both in a global sense and in a very personal sense; that there is an area left that needs to be healed.

The gift of two fingers to the heart, either done physically or etherically, will help in this healing. You are reaching out to the person with your index and middle finger, and you are touching their heart chakra. You are transmitting a laser beam of light from your heart to their heart; all the love you have, all the love you can channel from us, the Mother. It is a gift directly to their heart, particularly when you are not willing, or not yet ready to open and to receive back from the person. You send this beam into their heart, allowing the heart-opening to begin.

Having the soul conversations, speaking to the higher self, to the higher purpose, to what is truly going on, is also very valuable because it will be communicated from the higher universal self to the physical personality self; to the ego self; and into the integrated self at a rather rapid pace.

When it is truly a difficult situation, what we would recommend is that you speak in Perro. Perro is language with no charge or emotion attached; the language of straightforward information. Some of you may think of this as non-violent communication, but on a spectrum, non-violent communication is actually farther along. Perro simply means, "The facts, ma'am, nothing but the facts!"

As the relationship becomes a little bit warmer, better; when these tools that you are implementing are beginning to improve; you can use what we call the infinity. You begin the flow of the infinity, the sideways number eight, flowing from your heart to the other person's heart – collecting the information, the love, the color, the ray; bringing it back to your heart, and sending yours back out. This is particularly powerful in friendships and, of course, in sacred partnership. In this way you always remain in continuity.

You set the infinity to run constantly, twenty-four/seven. In that way you are connected and the flow of love between the two of you never stops. With what we would call a difficult situation or a difficult person, there has been a fracture or an injury. When you have that infinity flow it creates a mending of the fracture. You can have multiple infinities flowing at once.

The other last piece of this is: do not forget your sense of humor. Look at what you are really put off about and see the humor in it. See it with compassion; see it with my eyes, see it with the Mother's eyes. Be gentle, particularly with yourself. And smile, engage and love.

Unite With The Kingdoms

As stewards and partners with all life on Earth, the profound question is how best to embrace all the kingdoms on Gaia, including the plants, animals, and nature spirits. One of the ways you may begin this closer relationship with the various kingdoms is to invite those aspects of yourself to join within you, so that they are very clearly, consciously present. Remember what I have guided you in terms of embracing your aspects or working with difficult people. Utilize the same processes that I have described.

Ask for your fairy self, because she is more in touch with the elements, to come within you, or your leprechaun or your dwarf self. While everyone tends to migrate to the angelic or fairy self, there are many forms of elementals.

Ask them to come within and to make themselves known to you. Invite and become familiar, not only with your totems and familiars, but with your stones (you do not tend to think of yourself as part of the mineral kingdom, and yet of course you are). Determine which totems (animal spirits) or which stone or mineral you feel most closely aligned with. Have you invited the water sprites forward? Think of all the ways to engage with the seen and unseen realms of your beloved planet. Open and play with it!

What do I mean when I say, "Speed

up, slow down?" This exercise is best done outside. If you cannot physically be outside, you can place yourself at a window gazing outside. If you say, "I can't do that because I live in Manhattan and all I am gazing at is a brick or cement wall," don't forget the brick and the cement molecules are alive. But you can also just get yourself a picture of nature and gaze at that as well.

Slow down so that you are almost in a stillpoint, as quiet and as still as you can be. Of course we will help you and your plants, animals and trees will help you. What you do is simply rest in your heart but with your ears wide open, your chakras wide open (because these are all receptors), your third, fourth and fifth eyes all wide open, and your hands wide open. Remember, you receive information in such a variety of ways.

For example, choose your favorite tree. Ask the tree to communicate, and if you can lean against the tree or touch the bark while you are doing this, it is even better. The rhythm of the tree is very much like the long waves of sound, and what the tree has to say to you is not normally just a human conversation.

Begin the conversation by introducing yourself, ask the tree their name. Every being has a name and for them to share their name is a sacred gift. Then, simply ask them what they want, what they wish to share, what are their observations of how things are going in this shift of ascension, what are they feeling in the roots of Gaia.

Are the plates shifting? Is the earth moving? Are the ants nervous or are they busy building?

When you are speaking to other spirits and kingdoms, the frequency is very high; so it tends to be rather very high-pitched and very rapid. For example, some bushes, some grasses, some flowers will speak at a million-miles-per-hour. Ask them to slow down or ask yourself to speed up and to remember how to speak this language because it is already within you.

They have been waiting; they have been waiting eons for you to re-engage in this conversation and to really be in sacred partnership with you. The way a frog speaks to you is different than a way that a deer or a coyote speaks to you. The way a house cat speaks to you is different from a bobcat. Pay attention, and allow the undulations and the frequencies to reach you and then be translated into ways that you can understand.

Sometimes these communications will not be auditory; it will just be the deep connection and knowing, because that is how they do it. It is far more telepathic and unspoken, but you can hear the language as well.

Allow the bond between yourself and the myriad of kingdoms to expand. Talk to the mountains and the streams; dance with the fairies and the flowers; discover the mysteries of the caves and caverns. One of the greatest delights of being in form is the discovery and building of relationships with all the beings who cohabitate this wondrous planet with you. Open your heart, eyes, ears and sense of smell. Breathe in the essence of the Earth and allow the friendships to emerge and grow. Declare your love for all the kingdoms and they will join you gladly.

Stick Together

Each of your journeys is unique and magnificent, and yet at the same time, a small puzzle piece of the bigger unified whole.

I see many of you worrying about your mission: Am I doing it right? Am I letting anyone down? Have I fulfilled my purpose? Am I on track? I do not hear you say, Am I having fun? Do I feel loved? Do I love? Do I feel the connection to my family above and below?

One of the ways to maintain your highest vibration is to remind yourself, not only that you are not alone, but you are wholly and completely, without exception, loved.

You have been given many tools, and we could sit here and talk about prayer, ritual, meditation and esoteric studies. But I want to reach in and touch your hearts. This time of transition, of such massive change, when many old issues you thought you put to bed ages ago are coming to the forefront can be anxiety provoking and fearful. I want to touch your hearts and reassure you how deeply you are loved, because nothing main-

tains the highest vibration in the universe more than feeling, being, accepting and acknowledging love.

If I ever had one message to each of you, it is that you are love. It is the molecular structure of your being, the subatomic fibers of who you are; the light quotient. It is not something that disappears; it can't ever be taken from you. It is the core, essence and spark of you—unique and beautiful.

This truth has not been reinforced within most of you as you have been trained, brought up and educated. But there is a shift in your planetary humanness and you are becoming conscious of being love. You are more often choosing joy, choosing heart, choosing love. Yes, it requires diligence and practice, in the same way most things require practice. Many of you are just beginning to remember and relearn how to communicate with your hearts—how to be honest, truthful, trusting and hopeful in disclosing what is in your heart.

There is no being that came into a family without a soul agreement; yet, many of these soul agreements have been violated. If you are not fortunate enough to have family that understands who you are, and the fullness of your mission and purpose, I suggest that you take time to be with them, whether it is electronically, on the phone or in person. These people know and love you. They may not know the truth of everything, but even by being with them you are changing their vibration; this is entrainment.

I wish to share a couple of ideas and methods of how my Magdalena and I maintained clarity. The words "clarity" and "love" can be used in exchange for "high vibration" if that makes more sense to you.

One of the things we did was that we stuck together. When I say that, I mean that we spent our time with like-minded, like-hearted, like-believers: the disciples, the apostles, the many followers and friends—and that group grew exponentially every day. We would spend time with family, with those who knew our truth and who loved and accepted us for who we were and are. When you spend time—work time, play time, free time—with those who are like-hearted, like-minded, on the same journey, it reinforces you and gives you permission to be yourself.

When we would walk out to do the work, one of the things we would do would be to assess it beforehand. "Will this be reinforcing? Will this group be resistant? Do they believe in love? Do they believe in what I have to share?" If the answer was "yes" we would plunge right in, but when the answer was "no" we would do a great deal of preparatory work.

We would have soul conversations, we would send energy, we would ask the mighty ones, the archangels, to surround not only us, but them as well. We would use the tools at our disposal; we would prepare the way. Another thing we would do was create time for our sacred selves to do whatever we felt like doing. Sometimes, it was nothing except staring at the sky, playing with the baby, sitting quietly and sharing tea.

Sometimes it would be rich, deep, philosophical discussion to open our hearts and our minds even further, to bring that communion of all parts of ourselves. That is the gift of sacred union, of having one with whom you can truly share your hopes, fears, concerns and dreams. I know not all of you have been blessed in this way, but most of you have come with the intention, and therefore the plan, to have this experience of love.

Whether it is a community of thousands, a community of twelve, or a community of two, it is community and unity that helps to maintain the vibration. It is that sense of common mission, of being united in purpose, in belief and in knowing.

Home Is Where The Heart Is

I want to talk to you about home and homecoming. You have a saying, popular even in my time, that "Home is where the heart is." Also understand that heart is where your home is. It is where all love lives; it is where your essence emanates from, your divine expression of your magnificent sweet selves, as angels incarnate upon this planet.

In concert with many, I wish to reinforce you as you go forward in the next cycle of your existence, your soul journey and your

journey upon the planet. You need to be replenished in the way of laughter, joy, playfulness, and an understanding of your role and your responsibilities as we create and co-create with you the anchoring of Nova Earth, the cities of light, and whatever your heart desires.

My friends, no longer do I ask you to follow. I ask you to walk with me as teacher, as friend, as confidant, as family.

Many of you are isolated. As you begin this next cycle of existence, it is vitally important that you know, and have the support—not only of us—but of your friends and family, your soul family that travels with you.

As I have said to you so many times you must be sick of hearing it, my only message is love; that is all I have to offer. Oh, now and then a few loaves and fishes, a bit of healing where the recipient is willing, where the faith is strong—but all of that has emanated from love: love of yourself, love of each other.

You have acted as the embodiment, in human form, of love. I have been very busy working with you, and preparing you to

be an even greater embodiment—a greater vessel of that love, and that acknowledgment that you are love.

In that love, everything and anything is possible: whether it is the regeneration of a physical form, the regeneration of a broken heart, the regeneration of a family or of a community.

Where does it start? It starts in coming together to support and encourage, to laugh and play with one another. Share the energy of your sacred selves with each other. s I have with my apostles, my disciples, my family, realize that this is where your fuel and your support comes from. You will need it in the days ahead. No, it will not be Armageddon, but it will be busy.

There will be a gap, at times, in understanding between you, and you will need this support, this love, understanding, acceptance, allowance and nonjudgment of each other.

You need to share the miracles, to share the bread, and yes, sometimes the wine. You need to remember that you are one family, and you are my family.

CHAPTER 5
DIVINE UNION &
THE 13TH OCTAVE

This is the time of entry into the doorway. Long have I stood and awaited your arrival, for you are of the new nation. Each of you has come to brighten the day, to brighten the Earth, to carry the stars and to share the understanding of love. We have walked this path, my brothers and sisters, long ago and do so once again in fulfillment. It is a time of celebration, and I am pleased to welcome you home.

There is always balance of East and West, will and spirit, yin and yang, feminine and masculine. The only thing that is past duality is All. There is no room for the 'either-or' on your planet. There is no room for duality on any planet. You have asked whether the feeling of worthlessness pervades the entire universe. The answer is yes. That is why this Council of Love speaks of the introduction of love not just on this planet of Earth but everywhere, in all senses of existence and beyond. That is why so many have come to assist in her evolution and patterning, in her transformation of the grid.

The Miracle of the 13th Octave & Divine Union

What occurs in the heart of each one of you affects the entire collective. You think that you are a tiny group but you are now one circle, one spiritual community, united in heart. What happens here is felt far beyond what you can imagine. We tell you this not only to raise the remaining debris of fear, but that we may grab it from your stomach and soul, and disperse it. We tell you this so that you will know of your own infinity.

No spark of light, no essence of love is inconsequential. It is essential to the whole. It is essential to grow.

You have just begun your journey. We will walk with you again on this planet of Earth. We will talk often of this moment of union. We will share it with others and we will touch their hearts with the essence of purity and grace that rests within each one of you. It doesn't matter whether you are a scientist, what you deem to be a logical thinker. There are many of you who have been the scientists previously, and who have vowed to take a different route during this lifetime. Whether you are a ditch digger, a fisher of men, or an important president, you need to recognize the wondrous nature of your being. We have known your wonder for some time. So come home.

Know that you who have passed already through the 13th Octave doorway with James, my apostle - who have entered this sacred circle - have indeed changed. It is subtle, but not. Each of you assumes the mantle, the cloak for many who inhabit the Earth and who walk upon her. You are indeed the pathfinders. It is the pathway home to knowledge, to the heart of love.

The fear, addiction, and anxiety continue

to be released for your own selves, but also for those who travel in your wake. You release, and by doing so, assist those who follow you. This is a soul agreement—for many who wished to come forward have not done so because of their fear and lack of ability to clear. You are assisting those who wish to enter through the doorway, with their clearing of fear. It is a grave undertaking.

At the same time, you are entering into the 13th Octave energy to literally be in a state of divine union. You do this for those still engaged in the path of the old third dimension, and for those wishing to enter into the 13th Octave. It is extremely difficult to do this if you do not remain within the energy of the 13th Octave; otherwise the burden weighs you down enormously. This burden could bury you; it bears down upon you and wears you away. So it is important to be within the energy which is lighter, the energy of wholeness, of love.

All addictions to the third dimension, the old grids and false paradigms, must be released. That is accomplished from the place of the 13th Octave. That is done by manifesting in the seventh dimension, the place of heart. It is essential for all of you to anchor as firmly as possible within the thirteenth.

Many who are on this planet have been imprinted with false information. But do not forget that everyone has also been imprinted with the Divine Plan. It is a matter of stripping away all false interpretations, all misinformation, until all that is left is the kernel of truth for the integration of this purpose: for Earth to return to her sacred self, for each soul, each spirit who inhabits her, to become and to be this circle of the unity of spirit and body, of the will and heart, of the love. There is no room anymore, not on our side or within the universal blueprint, for the lack of understanding of this principle.

Each one who enters the doorway of divine union takes upon themselves this sacred rite of passage. You walk much as I have walked through the valleys, as Moses has walked long ago through the parting of the seas. There is no difference. It is a miracle of equal value, equal import. In the generations to come they will talk again of the original group who went to the desert to find water, for it is the water of life, the substance of spirit.

Will you allow yourself to enter back into this love?

Calm the Earth, for she is tremulous, and continue with all of your heart to believe. It is the way home. As we believe in you, we ask for your faith in the plan, in the restoration of love. We wish to lighten your hearts, brighten your souls, for as you have given to us, so we return to each one of your hearts a million fold. Do not step aside, but step in. Close your circle and make it airtight. You are blessed and you are holy.

The Doorway Beckons

The doorway to the 13th Octave of divine union beckons you. The opening has been accomplished through a miracle; a gift of love from our One Divine Being to your divine being, united in heart. It is our dearest wish that you enter. It is why you have prepared and endured all the trials, tribulation and chaos of this and many, many lifetimes.

The answers to universal questions that have plagued you lie beyond this gateway. This opportunity is unique in the experience of your planet. You are presented with an invitation engraved with the lettering of the celestial stars, the energy of the Divine. Those of you who intend to enter, know who you are, and will resonate throughout your entire being to this message.

The 13th Octave, the process of being in divine union, is beyond your concept of time or space; it is completely beyond your grid or the grid of physicality. It is beyond your dimension; it is the state of being united with All, which is all that ever could be, all that ever has been.

The cycle of the twelve existences, the twelve dimensions that the human race is able to experience will continue for the many on Earth who do not choose, or are not as yet prepared to enter this state of being. For those who have chosen long ago, who have been encoded with the genetic and soul desire to enter, the doorway is opened to the next level, the next circle.

One of the primary reasons for the opening of the doorway at this time is because of the spiritual progress and self-sacrifice of Earth. Through her mission of service, in harmony and in conjunction with those aligned with her energy grid, she has catapulted herself to the end of possible experience within your grid. She seeks entry to a new octave, a completely different realm of existence.

Her prayers have been heard and answered, and the doorway opened. Clear yourself of all blockages and debris, enter into the state of love and serenity, and align with the light. The doorway is opened and time, in the very practical sense of which it is applied on Earth, is of the essence. Earth exists in the seventh dimension and walks in an expanded reality.

When I spoke so long ago of love, it was never love of anything in particular, it was simply love. The time has arrived for the vibration of pure love to be permanently anchored upon this planet and within the hearts of all who inhabit her.

When you enter the 13th Octave, you unite with love, for that is all there truly is. From that place of expansion, those who enter through the gateway anchor even more firmly upon sweet Gaia to assist those who continue the path of 12:12 of the older form of human existence.

This choice of joining with Source will

not be the same as your earlier attempts of what you have felt as reaching out to God. As you re-anchor this purity of love, it is not only through your emotional, physical, or mental bodie—for these will be reunited, reintegrated with the whole. Your expanded self anchors back through the energy fields of the dimensions, back into the hearts of humans, animals, flowers—all beings—to touch their hearts, to brush them with the gentle knowing of love, to spark that essence within them that they may expand to the point of fully knowing the wholeness of the existence with One.

No, beloved, this does not mean abandoning your body. This does not mean dying and leaving all whom you cherish behind and bereft. This means allowing the fullness of your beautiful sacred self being fully expressed and fully present on Earth.

In the distant future there will be a time when all go to the 13th Octave. At that point, the planet and those upon it will simply become brilliant gold—sheer energy, sheer light—and it will be done.

It begins now with each of you and your decision, your expression of free will, of whether you choose to join with us in heart and love. All are welcome, all are told of the vision so they may also know that there is assistance, guidance and hope. It is the lack of hope, the lack of dreams, which have held so many on this planet away from love, away from the wholeness of their being—which has kept us in separateness.

Wholehearted surrender—not to God but to self—is necessary for divine union. It is the most selfish act and the most selfless undertaking. It is the leap of faith; it is the believing in the miracles of love with absolutely no evidence.

Those who have been chosen, who have nominated themselves long ago, are fully capable of this exit and entry. You are not alone. Look through the door; we all await you—yes, thirteen holy ones for certain, but also the entire Legion of Light. It is a welcome home party and all has been prepared. Afterward, you will go back through the door, altered and whole, to assist others in their journey. None will be left unaided; even those who refuse will be aided by the light penetrating the darkness until it no longer exists. There will be many miracles to observe. Prepare and enter.

Fear, Trust and Forgivenss

As I have told you, the gift upon returning from the 13th Octave will be simply touching another's heart, and having it healed.

However, movement through the energy field into the 13th Octave raises the most acute feelings of fear and insecurity in all of you. Long ago, I told you that the keys to heaven are trust and forgiveness. The keys to the 13th Octave are also trust and forgiveness.

The passage into the 13th Octave of divine union is a leap of faith—a separation from all you have known on this human plane of existence. I am asking you to take the giant step of forgiving all those who have caused you injury and grief not only during this lifetime, but for all lifetimes and all existences. This is enough to trigger anxiety and fear within your heart.

Yet, when that clearing has been completed, the forgiveness I ask you to extend is to yourself: to forgive yourself for all real or imagined grievances, to forgive yourself for all the perceived wrongs and failures you have, or believe you have committed throughout time.

Part of the process of preparation to enter the 13th Octave of divine union is the reintegration of the many denied aspects of self. As you reintegrate all your denied aspects, do not deceive yourself. There will be many aspects that you find distasteful and even despicable; that is why you have denied this aspect, this part of yourself, in the first place.

This denial was far more than uncomfortable; it caused such feeling of chaos within you that it was easier to deny than to accept, alter and change. Now, dear ones, the time has come to put aside those judgments of yourself and having done so, to leave this current plane of existence behind and enter a new state of being: the 13th Octave.

Understand that you cannot enter a state of wholeness with All that is and All that ever can be, with only a portion of self. Also understand that this undertaking has many, many rewards—the least of which is that you will reintegrate those aspects of yourself that you perceived as too outstanding and too stellar to maintain. Much of human experience is distrustful and disdainful of both extremes; the human race has come to be frightened by both.

This is ironic when one considers the original plan for Earth. The purpose was for pure unadulterated spirit to have the joy, the experience, of being in a physical body while maintaining their angelic knowing and wholeness. With entry into the 13th Octave, that purpose is restored and completed.

There are other issues that raise fear within your heart at the prospect of entry into the 13th Octave. The invitation requests that you leave all known planes of human existence at this juncture in the unfoldment of the Divine Plan. For some, the prospect of leaving all human experience and reality behind is appealing; there are those who have never adapted well to the human form.

But also understand that wishing to leave Earth is a form of denial—denial of your true spirit, whole and mighty, which has chosen to enter this reality and have this experience. This form of denial also must be cleared and eliminated prior to entry to divine union. You must first learn what it

134

is to exist wholly and completely within the human form while consciously maintaining your connection to the Divine.

Exiting the familiar realm and entering the 13th Octave is assured to raise fears from a cellular level. It speaks to the survival mechanism at the very core of your being, which is part and parcel of the human equipment—and indeed the equipment of all who walk on Earth.

This fear is further magnified by the leap of faith which will require you to leave that realm of existence behind while continuing to straddle realities, dimensions, and states of being. All the while, you continue your path of spirit and become a service worker for the rest of humanity—a humanity that does not genuinely have the capacity to comprehend your realm of existence or experience.

I assure you that the rewards of this union are many, and I will come and walk with you in the new way of being. But accept that inner voice which questions you and demands to know what assurances you have that this will transpire.

Understand that fear is the guardian of trust and forgiveness. It alerts your heart and soul that there are blockages that need to be addressed, a small child alone and frightened who needs to be reassured. Think if you were a helpless toddler and you were told that you needed to cross the continent alone to see your parents. Even if you were offered all assurances that you would be accompanied, escorted, and have every physical and security need addressed, you would still be in a state of trepidation.

Do not judge your fear. Thank it and ask its assistance in more clearly identifying those areas which need to be coddled and taken care of in order for you to be taken care of. Understand that fear occurs on many levels, from the cellular to the most complex system of spiritual existence.

You do not wish to extinguish your eternal flame—the fear is that basic and that complex. All you have to go on is trust, but you cannot fully trust until you have forgiven. The cycle of fear, trust, trust, fear is a mechanism to serve you, not defeat you. Accept that built-in mechanism; use it and go forward.

Throughout your life, you have always striven to help others—to understand them and to forgive them when they have consciously or unconsciously hurt you. You have tried to live my message of forgiving and doing unto others. But you have forgotten one essential piece of that teaching, one essential element of that practice.

You have forgotten to love and forgive yourself; all of yourself. To accept and allow yourself is to know not only the wonderful shining star you are, but all parts; warts and all. To love and cherish that thoughtless child, the ignorant fool, the critical cynic, the bitter heartless part of you.

It is my wish, and part of the Divine

unfoldment, that you love, forgive, and cherish all parts of you. All parts of an extension of the Divine must be called home, nurtured and loved so they can be made whole. What you deem and despise as the part of your being you wish to disown is the very part of you that I ask you, this day, wholly and completely, for all time and throughout eternity, to forgive.

Intentions are extremely important, but sometimes intentions and actions go astray. Very often it is how you have learned; it is part of the process of human existence. It is how you have come to know me, for I have always come for you in your darkest hours. Never think that I will desert you or will not be present exactly when you have need of me. When many have spoken of me as savior it meant helper, helpmate.

The promise I exact from you this day, and for all time, is to forgive yourself. Allow fear to be released, for there is no fear when you have felt my continued and continual presence and support. Release it now. Feel my lightness enter within you and warm your heart.

You are released from the fears and worry which can drown you. You are safe—all parts of you are safe and loved, cherished by your guides, this Council of Love, and me. Know this, trust this, and accept this forever. When you are willing and ready, allow yourself to enter my embrace as I take you home, into the 13th Octave—to your life, to your family, to your heart.

The End of Separation

We have walked in many lifetimes across the deserts and plains and spoken of this time of wholeness, of family reunion, where all the distant cousins and tribes would gather from all points on this globe. This is that time, this is that day.

The time is now. I am in your midst. You can see my face; you see it when you look in the mirror, and you see it when you gaze in the eyes of another, for this is our sacred purpose, to understand that we are One. Children of the Mother, children of the Earth, let us play.

Know that as we walk in union with All, that the tasks will grow. This is the beginning. This is why we have spoken of your need for miracles, which is simply magnification of trust through the heart of One. Here you are being challenged; you are being invited to come within to the union places, to the four corners of your heart.

The teachings of all paths and disciplines, what has come to be known as religion, is simple—it is to open your heart and love. Not simply to love one another, to love this planet of green, or self, but to be the love, to become embodiment of this way of existence. It is necessary to enjoy the physical presence that you have been given.

When we speak to you of the end of the separation, layering, duality, of light and dark; it is in order that you may enter and embrace the wholeness of love. When you live in heart, you live in root and crown. There is no difference. I work with you, as we all do, for indeed the entire Council of Love works as one. Each of you has attending spiritual physician to help clear the last fear of separation so this illusion may go and fly with the dove. It's time. This is the step you have yearned for, and one of the sole (soul) reasons you are upon Earth.

When we speak of soul mission, it is in reference to your unique sparks of light, gifts and abilities. In your own unique way, each path, each expression is a blessing that you offer from your heart to all. That is what you do when you touch the heart of another. You give them your heart, which is expanded in love. You give them the joy of knowing the fullness of who you and they are. Play my children, for it is a time of laughter, a time of joy, and a time of peace.

The Permanent Opening

Each of you has known me in many ways and times, past and future. We have traveled the universe together. We have walked upon this planet of brown and green, blue and gold. Variety was one of the riches of original form, the unlimited possibility to experience love, whether it was in the form of flower or mountain, healing being or furry friends. I have come to you through the doorway, for the preparation is complete.

Know that you began your entry into the 13th Octave, eons ago. That is why for many of you there is a knowing or familiarity with this term, a deep desire to reconnect with this energy of divine union. This is a promise you made to yourself long ago, and one you were aware of when you chose to return to Earth during this time of change. You knew this process of divine union would be available to you in form and knew not only how precious and extraordinary this gift is, but how it would assist you and many in the reanchoring of love upon Earth.

It is also time my friends, to come home to your heart, to come home not only to our love but yours. Within each of you rests the golden flame, a spark of Oneness. You journey with us to expand this spark into a blazing inferno that all can see; that all you encounter on all planes and dimensions will be part of your inferno. It is a cozy fire to warm their souls and to light the way. You have chosen to be the pathfinder, each in your own specific way. You have come to know this clearly, eager to gather further details during this time.

Your presence is melded with your circle and with we who are the keepers of the doorway to the 13th Octave of divine union. Now that you enter through the doorway to the 13th Octave, never again will it be closed to you or anyone who seeks it. With the anchoring of Archangel Gabrielle's golden spiral of light, upon which you ascend into the heart of One and descend back into physicality, you anchor the love permanently, and we go forward together. We bless you and embrace you. Each of you is sacred soul.

My blessing to you this day is the gift of love. Focus within your heart, for this is where we live with you. Focus upon that which you most dearly desire, a single thing, and we will magnify it together. I request that you allow me to infuse you as we walk together again on this planet.

Come Home

We come together to bring you and thousands, millions home to the heart of One, the heart of All. We have joined in union long ago and now simply continue. You come to be initiated into the 13th Octave to anchor love upon this planet. You do so with the assistance of my beloved brother, and your friend, our apostle James.

Many of you have felt my presence near and far, and I tell you that I walk with you now and always. It is not in some distant future that we tread this physical planet of Earth together again. I ask you to come to me and join in fortitude and courage with mercy and awe. There are many among you who have always chosen to work with the downtrodden in the places of chaos. It is your chosen passage to touch the hearts of many throughout the entire universe for none of you is limited by geography.

All is prepared. Come home with me, for you are ready and I am waiting.

Holy Spirit & Will

The Holy Spirit does not partake of form. Even the symbols used and assigned are not fully representative. The Holy Spirit is an essence and the divine spark of One. It is the inspiration and is very closely aligned not with love, but with will.

I have spoken to you many times of the need for love. Love of self is, indeed, love of another. In this world, this spark of inspiration fuels the need for direction, physical action and participation. This is where the Holy Spirit truly speaks to you, and where many of you have avoided going. Yet this partnership, this intertwining of will and love, is absolutely essential.

When you are asked, "What do you wish; what do you will; what is your inspiration?" Do you allow yourself to receive the Holy Spirit within? What you are being asked is, "What has been encoded within you, by you, prior to coming?" Your will is directing what you wished to accomplish upon the Earth—and your partner is Holy Spirit. You are not independent; we are linked. Think of us as having our hands intertwined; to do so, both sets of hands are necessary.

You know the Holy Spirit. You have been visited by this energy time after time; it has lifted and inspired you. There is a matter of trust. You are being asked to step forward, and you have the will to do this; you always have.

You have received the original flame of the Holy Spirit. It is one of your symbols, a part of your heart; it is part of that spark and golden flame that I have spoken to you about. It is the flame of the Spirit. Yet you ask yourself time and time again, "Is this so?" This flame is emblazoned within you. This is not a burden; this is an honor. You need not trust in me or Spirit or God. You need to trust your sacred self.

The Godhead is infinity, beyond comprehension. It is universe upon universe without end, encompassing all. Often, you have given God a face so that you feel comfortable. But it is not a face—human or otherwise. It is love. This is the essence of the energy of the universe; this is what you are invited to participate in.

How you do this is to take the love and direct it through an act of will. I never asked you to sit here on Earth and twiddle your thumbs. I ask you to be women and men of action—to make your life a living breathing energy that accompanies you in everything you do, from brushing your teeth to conquering Everest.

It is not enough to sit at home and just feel the love. Service and action need to be exhibited, not only with those you cherish, but with those you think you despise—for they are your deepest friends. They show you the most brilliant mirror of who you truly are.

You have been given your gifts, your talents: art of hand, art of mind, art of home and sacred space. Use them as a demonstration of who you are. You look for miracles in the sky. Each time you act out of love, directed by your own sweet self, you are performing a miracle. And, each time you just go through the routine as drudgery, you are denying who you are. You may deny this to yourself, but we know you. I know you. As a brother, I will remind you who you are. You are the one I love.

Gather your energies in your heart. This is particularly important for many who live hovering in the ethers. You need to pull your energy down all the way through you, and then up to your heart. Many of you have lived through your creative force and your creative being—it is time to join them within the heart center, the new balance point of Nova Being and New Earth.

This does not mean to ignore the chakras of your being; for each center is a unique gift. My Mother spoke of passion; it is fuel, as is laughter and joy. You need to live fully in your physical form. Use the gift of your brain for it is a mighty tool, but it is not the master of all. It needs to be consulted, not rule demonically.

Often you experience the Holy Spirit as waves of extreme heat. That is one of the ways in which you know it is the energy of the Holy Spirit. A lot of activation taking place at this time is literally coming through the back of your chakras and of your being.

139

Many of you will experience the openings at the back of your head, your neck, and the back of your heart and harmony chakras because it is easier to access. We are literally setting you on fire.

Similarly, many of you are experiencing this ignition all the way down your spine, particularly in your lower chakras. At the same time as you are being open fully to the intelligence of your heart—not simply the intelligence and knowing of your mind—you are also being opened at root to the kundalini, to the passion of the physical body, to the passion of living in physical form.

Many of you will feel a physical shifting and awakening that you have not felt in many years. Try not to freeze up. Simply relax. Tell yourself that you are being activated, and welcome it. It is simple, and it is done. It is a heart thought, not a mind thought.

Drop into your heart and say, "Thank you." When it is too intense, ask for it to ease; not for the energy, but for the neuromuscular electromagnetic impulses to soften. At times, you are so eager to welcome the energy that you overdo it, and simply over excite the physical form.

Rant and rave, but not from your head. Let go. I will catch you as I have caught you many times. This business of trying to live is not a matter of earning your worth, of paying off debt. It is a matter of reaching that point where you simply say, "All I can do is be."

Divine union is a heart surrender of love and will. Don't worry about feeling exhausted or empty. The emptiness is the blessing. It is then you are refilled with new life, new inspiration, and new well-being. So when you think you have tried and tried and tried, and you are fed up to here, do not cry, "Uncle!" Cry, "Jesus!" I will be there.

Part of this new energy that we speak of: the birthing of the new consciousness, the expansion of heart and mind in tandem and cooperation, the infinity sign that flows between you and All and every other being on Earth and far beyond, the space that you hold of divine connection, in service to yourself and others is what people call the Christ consciousness.

It is love. It has never changed. It is simply being fully in and of you. It is not gaining anything; it is simply finding it within, which is why I ask you to go inside and dream your dream. Discover what is still blocked and release it; give it to the Mother and Father. Give it to me. Embrace back unto yourself every aspect, every particle, and every piece of who you are and who you have ever been and who you ever will be.

Then we will come, and we will walk. It will not simply be me, Jesus, but many. And it will be North and South and East and West. The circles will form and reform, and dance across the globe. We will come as partners, each bringing gifts. We do not come to be lords and masters. We come to be servants, brothers, and partners. Many of us will walk this earth again in celebration.

Ascension & The 13th Octave

I welcome you into the 13th Octave. This is a sacred prayer and ritual that has been gifted to humanity in preparation for this time of ascension. No, it is not ascension, because it is intended in ascension that you will become the fullness of your transdimensional self and will anchor within the reality of the seventh dimension; completely and wholly in the heart of love, in the power of Creation.

This prayer, dear one, is to unite your being, your essence, and your soul within the Heart of One, so that conscious awareness, your sense of wholeness, is completely aware. In this, you also receive all the gifts of the 13th Octave; most importantly, the Thirteen Blessings and Virtues, also known as the Divine Qualities, upon which Nova Earth is built and anchored.

I am asking each of you not only to come with us but to bring your family, your friends, and if you have the heart, those that you consider the most resistant—and to continue to do this, for it helps with everybody going through this ascension portal.

Once they are reconnected to the love, they will wish to ascend. The fear will be eliminated; it is that simple. I also want you to know that all the kingdoms of Earth,

the ones you so often think of as "not hearing"—the mountains, trees, dogs, cats, coyotes, elephants—are all coming with you. It will be quite a parade!

I welcome you. I am with you in this journey of Oneness, in this journey of unity, connectedness and balance.

Union

It is time for all above and below, within the heart of your mother planet and within the heart of the Universal Mother to celebrate. This is my message for you my friends who have anchored the many rays for many species and in so doing have anchored yourselves with a glistening array of rainbow colors which is a delight to the eyes.

Know that the whale and dolphin sing the triumph of their union with you. In assisting your friends of the water, you have penetrated the heart of the Mother. Your friends move from plain to plain upon the back of the unicorn to carry the magic forward to all who wish to receive. Always it has been a matter of choice and never more so than now.

Your family of the 13th Octave opens their hearts further to expand and hold vibration for the planet and universe, and for themselves and you beloved one. The circle of the thirteen Ascended Masters, the legions of light and this entire Council of Love has expanded magnificently. Now it is your turn. You are in the company of those who love you, who have always loved you and who come in service and in peace, not the peace of the dead, but the peace of the living.

This expansion is the sound of harmony. It is the magic of knowing that you may travel to the deepest part of the ocean, the deepest part of yourself, to the depths of the universe, and reemerge with access to All. This is the miracle as promised. But most of you have not fully accessed the treasure house of reserves. This is not said in any way as criticism, it is said as invitation to come and claim your prizes.

There will be moments, solemn and heavy, as final releases are made. Attend to those who now emerge from the center of the Earth, and those from above who bring new delights. You go forward together as one circle intertwined with us to infinity for all eternity, and you will know me when I speak.

I join with you in sacred union, in divine union, in body, soul, and purpose. Many Earth changes come to pass in different forms. As your hearts open and shift, so does the heart of Gaia, for she understands that many send her the love and energy of renewal. It is not only the task of Gaia to take care of fear and anger, suffering and pain upon this Earth. That is also our undertaking; to assist each being born into human form to recognize their essence of love. This 'absence of knowing' is unique

to your race on Earth. All other species and life forms are aware. That is why animals transmute so clearly and quickly.

As I return, my message remains the same, it is about love. I will not return in war time strife and poverty, but in the abundance of riches not material. My friends, you will clothe and house me, feed and nurture me, and walk with me again as soul-mate and soul brother. We will share a joke and witness the miracles together. I have no desire to do this alone and neither do you. So, we will return as group, as a circle, and be known clearly: This will not be a mystery guest appearance.

You know me by the touch to your heart. You have begun your transfer to the seventh dimension through the 13th Octave, through the heart of One. That is my home and that is where you will find me. You see me often in meditation, but I also wish to be seen with open eyes, in laughter, union and beauty of love. I am with you, go in peace.

The Gift of Heart Healing

Fear not, you hear my messages clearly and you need to speak and share it throughout many lands. When you speak of the 13th Octave and you do not receive a response, this is a signal from me; the message sent directly to you, that heart healing is necessary. It doesn't matter whether you focus on healing the leg, the eyes, the heart or the healing of the universe. All is heart healing, and that is all that is required.

And how do you do this? By allowing the love within you, sent to you, and part of you, to be communicated to that cell. All people wish and desire to live in love, yet many of you ultimately live in misery, with a lack of self-worth and loneliness. You have the gift, opportunity and understanding to heal hearts. I will walk with you to do this, but you also physically walk alone.

Yet at the same time, it is time for us to return again. That is why we speak of the union of One. It is part of our unfoldment as well. For always we have wished to be in your presence, as you have wished to be in ours. Not in the unseen manner, but in the manner of physical friends as well. Like your friends from the outer reaches, we come in love to replace any and all pain, to rebirth the planet. Allow your light to burn brightly, your vibrancy to shine.

When you are going before the public, you carry the essence of All, so know that your screen will be crowded. It is not the words. It is the vibration and the light that is present in your face, your aura, your smile, your eyes, in the words that are thoughtfully chosen to show that you are awake. You reflect that choice to live in a manner that is demonstrative of love, that never belittles another, that is always compassionate, that always takes into consideration not what you know, but what the others do not know; what they have need to learn and receive. If you always think of this and ask in prayer, prior to any engagement, for it to reach all, to give each being that which they most desperately seek; you will never, ever go astray, and you will awaken millions. Your undertaking is large, but you do not go forward alone.

Celebrate

I have always loved celebration where love is shared. I do not come to this world ever again to wear a crown of thorns. I will always turn the other cheek, but understand, sometimes this is simply so the person will not see me laughing, for this is what you do. It is absurd that one human being would believe they can really hurt another. It is impossible.

You often think regarding the fulfillment of your mission on Earth, "What should I do? How should I perform? Where should I go? How should I live? With whom should I live? How to decorate?" On and on, and I say, do exactly what you want to do. Go where your passion and your heart are, where your joining with me has occurred. There is need for infinite variety of service upon this beautiful planet. The most important gift that you may give would be to do nothing when you feel like it. We have done this before.

We can walk an extra mile, but not ten. Relax. It is not that there is enough time. It is that there is no such thing as time, and the time is right now. You are only effective in your purpose, which is my purpose, when you touch others in love. Whether you touch their minds, bodies, or spirits, you are touching their hearts. Know that when you touch another, you touch me.

I will walk among you and I do not wish and will not be surrounded by friends who are anything other than playful. Your world is surrounded by your stars that wink at you, by dolphins who play with you, by whales that sing to you, by dogs that smile. Follow them as I do. Receive the gift of vision. Expand your gifts of knowing and enter the 13th Octave, not alone but with me, into the dance of joy.

Spin and fly with me now, and see me now. There is one existence and it is love.

CHAPTER 6
THE BLESSINGS

Long ago, in what you have come to call the Sermon on the Mount, I have shared with you some of the blessings of the Father for those who are true to love and to the Word. The blessings of the Father are infinite and eternal. Understand, none who turn to Him are turned away. None who seek are not guided towards the truth of that love. None who sit alone in the darkness are ever forgotten. None who cry out from the depth of their loneliness are not heard. None who serve are overlooked and forgotten. All are heard, all are rewarded, all are received back into the heart of One.

The Beatitudes

I spoke these words (Gospel of St. Matthew 5:3-12) so you would understand and remember the infinite love of our Father:

"Blessed are the poor in spirit,
theirs is the kingdom of heaven.

"Blessed are the meek,
they shall inherit the earth.

"Blessed are they who mourn,
they shall be comforted.

"Blessed are they who hunger and thirst for what is right, they shall be satisfied.

"Blessed are the merciful,
they shall have mercy shown them.

"Blessed are the pure in heart,

they shall see God.

"Blessed are the peacemakers,
they shall be called children of God.

"Blessed are they who are persecuted in the cause of right, theirs is the kingdom of heaven.

"Blessed are you when others abuse you and persecute you and speak all kinds of evil against you for my sake. Rejoice, and be glad, for your reward will be great in heaven; this is how they persecuted the prophets before you."

The New Beatitudes

Now, my beloved brothers and sisters, I add these words so that you of the twenty-first century will also remember that your words, actions and faith are always blessed. Understand my beloveds, this is the short list.

Blessed are the mothers,
they will be the children.

Blessed are the fathers,
they will know honor.

Blessed are the nurturers,
they will be nurtured.

Blessed are the providers,
they will be provided for.

Blessed are the pure,
they will be blessed with grace.

Blessed are the warriors,
they will find peace.

Blessed are the brave,
they will be defended.

Blessed are the truth-speakers,
they will be rewarded.

Blessed are the journalists,
they will be heeded.

Blessed are the writers,
they will be heard.

Blessed are the healers,
they will be healed.

Blessed are the teachers,
they will learn.

Blessed are the artists,
they will be in beauty.

Blessed are the ministers,
they will be attended.

Blessed are the leaders,
they will be led into the kingdom of heaven.

Blessed are those who forgive,
they will be forgiven.

Blessed are those who trust,
they will be reunited.

Blessed are the peacemakers,
they will be victorious.

Blessed are the disenfranchised,
they will be free.

Blessed are the beggars,
they will be showered with riches.

Blessed are the playful,
they will be in joy.

Blessed are the humble,
they will be raised up.

Blessed are those with patience,
they will be eternal.

Blessed are the quiet,
they will hear silence.

Blessed are those who suffer in the darkness of despair, they will receive the eternal light of hope.

Blessed are the doubters,
they will find faith.

Blessed are those who thirst for freedom,
they will be liberated.

Blessed are those who hunger for justice,
they will behold the truth.

Blessed are the truth seekers,
they will be revealed.

Blessed are the kind of heart,
they will receive infinite consideration.

Blessed are the merciful,
they will receive mercy

Blessed are the wretched,
they will be comforted.

Blessed are the despised,
they will be embraced by God

My beloveds, the love of the Father knows no bounds. There is infinite room in the Father's heart for all His children. None are excluded. Turn to Him and know the comfort and support of His infinite love. Let your light shine that all may see your good works for it is the reflection of your devotion to our Father. It is the reflection of infinite love.

The Gift of Purity

I came to Earth and joined with all of you on this beloved Gaia for one reason and one reason alone. I came to be the teacher, the vessel and the conduit of love. That is the only message and the only mission I have ever had. And, my beloved friends, it is truly the only journey and the only mission and purpose you have.

This mission of love, this experience, this opportunity to embody love, is a gift. Yes, at times it is a hardship because you make it so; at times it is ecstasy because you allow it to be truth. It has many faces, and each and every one of you has a unique expression of how that mission and purpose comes forward.

There is no difference, and there never has been, between your mission and my mission, my journey and your journey, my undertaking and your undertaking. The experience of my life as Jesus is somewhat different from yours because of time and space and culture, but when you scratch the surface it is the same.

It is incarnating and having the experience of connection and knowing of One—most particularly of the Mother but certainly the Father as well, because they cannot and will not be separated.

It is having the human experience of family, of friendship, and of finding the mission, path, and expression of service—along with the pitfalls and blessings within that. I never designed my life to be, or to be viewed as one of suffering and pain, loss, sacrifice, devastation. That was not the message I came to bring; it was not what I came in form to share. It was about love.

It seemed so simple, and yet it has turned out to be the most complex message to truly incorporate, understand and embody. Sometimes I hear you as you speak to me, plead to me, scream at me, saying, "Love, love, love, love! That is all you ever speak about! That is all the Council of Love ever talks about! That is all you care about!" You know what, dear hearts? You are absolutely right.

That does not mean that I do not understand about the journey of being in form; about life and the intricacies of what is contained within that simple word "love," within those simple words of "Love yourself" and "Love your neighbor."

This, my friends, is a time of new beginnings, of interdimensional reality, of the shift in consciousness—not only of the planet and the kingdoms, but of the entire human collective. What is this based on?

I can assure you it is not based on the old paradigms of the third dimension. Have those desolate qualities of greed and control, pain and suffering, lack of love, lack of worth, lack of knowing acted well as a springboard for each of you in your hearts to say, "Enough! I can tolerate this no longer?" Yes!

You are declaring that you desire love. So many of you are engaging not only in sacred partnership with us and your sacred self, but also with your divine partners, your family, your parents, your children, your siblings, your soul family.

You are declaring yourself, and what you are doing is monumental. You are saying, "I choose a world, a reality, which is the full experience available to humanity." The building blocks of this—the fibers, the molecules, the subatomic particles, are love. You are declaring that, and you are saying, "I deserve, I welcome, and I am, love."

It has never been sufficient to believe that you love another or that you love yourself. It is being, embodying and acknowledging that which you are. Your core essence, that spark of what you call light and I call divinity is love.

In that deep surrender, you open the floodgates to the totality of who you are, and to the meaning of your entire journey and that of every other being on Earth. It opens the floodgates for you to truly see, to know the truth of existence. In that opening, you are jumping through the portal.

Some of you would say to me, "Jesus, we have been waiting for the tsunami of love. We have been waiting for this or that event. We have been waiting for the opening of the floodgates." I am here this day to open those floodgates, heart to heart to heart to heart.

The darkness has reigned too long. It has given magnificent detail to the light, but there is truly, simply no room for what has been known on Earth, on Gaia, as the darkness. It hinders not only the Mother's Plan, but your plan.

When I walked the Earth, I knew very clearly—not always cheerfully, but certainly clearly—of my plan and my promise to the Mother. You do as well. In that plan, in your life, have there been deviations? Have you been sidetracked from time to time? Perhaps. But it doesn't matter. You are released from that and you are free.

The declaration for all beings of Earth to reanchor their purity is a decree of the Mother. I have brought the gift of Karmic Dispensation to the planet, through my gift of dying on the cross. When I have cried out, **"Father, forgive them, for they do not know what they are doing." (Luke 23:34), I have meant all who have sinned, erred or lost their way.**

So listen what I say to you now on behalf of the Mother as She continues to send you Her purity and clarity. She has decreed through the desire of Her being and Her infinite creation, the restoration of purity, of grace. The perceived absence of purity on Gaia in the human race has been a grand debate for a long time and rather futile, because that perception is filled with judgment and hatred. When the Mother decrees, when the Father/Mother/ One creates this restoration, it matters not if you have wandered off track. The only thing that is required is not forgiveness from above or below (not even from Gaia, for she has forgiven as well). The only thing remaining is forgiveness of your beloved self and your beloveds.

When you accept and anchor this energy of purity, this gift that is beyond naming, then you shift; your consciousness elevates. This is happening even as I speak with you. It has been happening as you have been subtly and actually following the Mother's suggestion to fall in love with each other. You cannot do that, not truly, not fully, until you have become the love.

That, my friends, is what ascension has always been about. It has had many labels and tags hooked on to assist in the understanding of what your Nova Earth and Nova Being look like: How you operate, how you feel. But it is all about love.

I know, in human time, it has felt like a millennium. I know what that feels like, and this is rapid!

You ask, "What should I do, then?" Go into your heart and explode with love. Don't wait, because the energy, the tsunami of love, is not only at your front door but in your kitchen, bedroom, basement, and attic.

It is not a tsunami of destruction. The only thing it washes away is the old that no longer serves you. It is refreshing. The water is clean and pure, and restorative. When the Mother says this is a time of recovery, this is what she is talking about.

Archangel Michael has spoken to you, and he has said, "None of you are junior carpenters." I have played that role. It was primarily to learn humility, for there were times when I was full of myself. You are not here to play an insignificant role. You are here in your mastery; not subservient, but with me, with all of us, to live the fullness.

We have all waited: St. Germaine, Sanat Kumara, the Buddha, El Morya and the Magdalena. We've waited for this time of reunion. Some of you may have forgotten, but before you came, you were fully aware that this was the time of reunion, not just ascension.

When you are in your fullness you are free to have us walk, talk, and continue to lift you up. That is the Plan.

Let Truth Flow

I am brother of your heart and brother of your soul. I come forth this day simply to hold you, to walk and be with you, to encourage you.

The words of truth must be heard. Very seldom will you hear me use the word 'must.' I use it because of the rapidity of the changes that are taking place, the benchmarks and the catalysts. The catalysts, dear friend, for the completion of this shift are the words of truth, and the emotion and actions of love. What else is there?

When I have walked the Earth, I daresay that my words were not always popular; they certainly weren't always politically correct. There were times when either my mother or Magdalena, my beloved one, would say to me, "Can't you just keep your mouth shut?" Sometimes I would even say it to myself, but I couldn't, because that was why I walked Earth; it was to talk about the truth. The truth isn't about war or money, greed or lust, political or biblical hierarchies. It's about love. It's about healing through love. It's about sharing with love. It's about tearing down the old and allowing the new to emerge. My beloved ones, that is exactly what you are doing. How you do that is through the speaking of truth.

Truth is always tempered with compassion. I have observed some people on your human plane who say, "Well, it's only the truth, and it is so cruel." That is not what truth is. Truth is a reaching out. It is looking at the divinity. It is looking at the mirror in the person who is so unlike you, and looking at that mirror until you see clearly that you are looking at me; you are looking at you; and you are looking at All. This shift is not about who is right and who is wrong. It is not about who has the best information. It is about love. This has never changed.

So what I ask of you, my brothers and sisters, is for you to join with me and to let me join with you during this time together, in love. Let all the self-criticisms go. Let all the judgment go. And allow yourself to be

who you are, because I know you. I know what you are capable of, and I know what you are capable of creating. Often you will underestimate yourself, but I never do. You have held the center for so long; you will not give up now. I welcome you and I ask of you: Let the truth flow. Let go of your mind and your ego, and let the truth flow. Go in peace.

Compassion

You've asked, "How do you heal?" I heal and I healed with love. It is the fuel of everything. It is the instantaneous recognition by both parties, by you and by the one you either glance at or touch, that they are completely loved. Their every fiber, atom and subatomic particle is moved and filled by love.

When that instantaneous transmission takes place, healing occurs. It need not take longer than an instant. You may spend an hour with your friend, but the healing is instantaneous. That transmission is the acknowledgement of the perfection of God. It does not stop; it is only interrupted by human ego. When you send and ignite that vibration of love it is done. It does not take hours or days; you do not have hours or days, nor do I ask you to take that much time.

I walk with you as brother, not as one who is ascended or favored. I walk beside you as one who loves you. When you have that moment of hesitation that even I have experienced, feel my hand upon your chest and let me remind you of the strength, compassion and love that I hold for you, that I give freely to you.

My friend, I have walked the Earth as man, prophet and sinner. Do you know how many times I have been called blasphemer? It is funny; it is ironic. Respond to those who swear exactly the same way I would, because they are in the desolation of their own despair. Love them, bless them, and hold compassion for them – for they cannot see. That is a terrible way to live, and it is exclusive to the human form.

I embrace you with my strength. It is a gentle strength, but is unbreakable. It is not brittle or demanding. It is able to flex where it has need to, for what is compassion except flexibility?

Compassion is the ability to extend yourself to yourself, to others, to your collective, to your world. It is the ability to understand what is being experienced without assuming the energy of that experience. With that understanding you send love, support and gentle strength in ways that help, support, soothe, comfort and nurture.

Changes are prominent and underway upon the planet in the birthing and anchoring of Nova Earth. Expand your hearts and minds to look at all humanity—to each being who is suffering in one way or another.

Many of you have studied and say,

"Suffering is a choice, Master." Yes, part of suffering is a choice; part of it is sometimes in the Divine Plan—either of the soul, the individual or the group. But I say to you, "Where is the compassion in such a statement?" Is it not sad that any being—consciously, unconsciously, or in accordance with God—would choose suffering? For even when it serves and teaches, it hurts!

Do you think that when I watched so much suffering as I walked the Earth, that it did not touch my heart? Of course it did. It did not disable me, but the compassion led me to my healing ministry.

Do not think it did not hurt when they flogged me and laid the thorns upon my head. Yes, it was in divine order and was my choice to endure, but I also know each one of you had compassion, and still do, for that situation. So why would it be any less for any human being who suffers; especially those who suffer alone in the dark, who do not know that they are loved and supported, who do not see the faint light of hope?

Send the energy of compassion and love around the globe. Let them know of your love, and let them know of your compassion. Send the love, compassion and strength to continue on. Love heals; that is all there is. There is no trial, no tribulation that cannot be healed; no dream, no creation that cannot be brought forth through the power of love.

Do not limit what you know to be true. Our Almighty Mother and Father are powerful beyond any imagination, and the power is sweet, gentle, and pervasive. Do not be modest in your prayers and your requests, and do not forget those who are in pain and suffering: a child in Africa with no clean water, the young man in prison with no dream of the future, the mother who does not have enough money to buy milk, the father who does not know whether he can pay the mortgage, the young woman who dreams of love, the old man who waits for his children to come.

Include them in your prayers; give them your compassion, your strength and love, and then give it always to yourself. I have need of you.

You are so deeply loved, beyond measure. You judge yourselves, but I know you: I know your magnificence, your flame, your soul, your history. I trust you, and I entrust you with this task.

There is no victory of peace where there is separation. When you send this love and compassion, it heals separation, dissolves it.

Go with my ever present love and compassion.

The Gift of Passion

I come to speak about passion; something often overlooked, underrated and underpaid. My beloved friends and family, my brothers and sisters of all rays, all colors, all lineages, what is life without passion?

What is love? Love is a passion. It may express as quiet or even silent, as meek and mild, or as outrageous and screaming for joy!

Each of you is the embodiment of the Mother and Father's passion, and even my passion. You did not come to this planet, nor did I, to lead a ho-hum boring life; quite the contrary—especially because you have incarnated at this time of such spectacular change.

There is nothing meek and mild about these extraordinary changes. Although it snuck up in the quiet of the night when you weren't looking, the energy that is sent to each and every one of you upon the planet at this time is filled with passion. It's passion for the unfoldment of the Mother's Plan; passion to see the fulfillment of Her Dream, our dream and your dream; passion to liven up your body, your life, your sacred unions with yourself and each other.

What is passion, and why is it linked to compassion? They are part of the same body. Passion is caring. It is the fire of action, intent. It is the ability to truly move in meaningful, directed, specific action. It is the ability to be the participant and the observer.

Passion is about a depth of caring, of acknowledging what is truly important, not merely in the global or the universal sense, but what is important to you. It is when you declare that you feel passionate about your beloved; or that you are passionate about a cause; or you are passionate about a belief.

But what does that really mean? It means that you care so deeply, that you love so deeply, so consistently, and might I even say, irrevocably. So, when you are truly in passion, it is not, "Oh, I feel passionate about this person, or that cause, this week." No, that is not passion; that is moodiness.

Passion is what you carried with you when you came to Earth. You, like we, carried the passion for the fulfillment of the Mother's Dream, the unfoldment of the Plan, the ascension of humanity, the embodiment of love; you held passion for what was possible.

Too often, passion is conceived or misconceived as inappropriate, fiery, not thought-out, unfelt-out, not caring about the consequences, outcomes or the affects of one's actions or thoughts. That is not passion; that is an abuse of free will and misdirected energy.

Passion is considerate, caring, serene—and it is the Fourth of July, Christmas, and New Year's Eve, and every occasion you can think of throughout the entire planet and far beyond in terms of fireworks, beauty, and excitement that is based on the fulfillment of love. You would not be here—and let me even be more clear—you would not be here still if you were not passionate, holding the passion for what is unfolding and coming. If you did not care you would say, "Far too much chaos, I'm out of here. Take me home." But you do care!

Yes, there have been times when you have felt that you have only endured. You have certainly carried valor, consistency and fortitude. But awe and wonder are part of passion. It is that sense of outrageous possibility and actuality because you can see, feel, and know what is inside that sensation—that feeling and knowing of what can be.

Passionate anchors in the present moment but it is, at the same time, very much part of the Mother's New Time because it is future directed as well. You don't get passionate about something that has already occurred, although you may carry the passion of that situation forward.

The energy which is being sent to all upon this planet by the Mother's legions, is a legendary move to clear, prepare, and in many ways push forward the unfoldment of Her Plan. It is passion; it is joy; it is a sense of knowing that you are exactly where you need to be—in the truth and the might of who you are.

I give you the gift of passion. I ask each of you to allow either the reignition or deeper ignition of passion—not only for the unfoldment, but for yourself; not only for what you think of as your divinity, but for every fiber of your being. Be passionate about the hair on your head, the nails on your hands, every part of your being. Because if you don't care deeply, then why bother? And if you don't care deeply, don't bother! Go to what ignites you; in this, we anchor the interdimensional Nova Earth.

In this together, my brothers and sisters, we fulfill the Mother's Plan; we bring to fruition Her Dream of love in form. I join you now; let us walk together.

Courage

I want to talk about gentleness, courage and stamina. This is quite a combination, is it not? The world you are living in, this Nova Earth that you and we are anchoring and co-creating, is also a place where there is turmoil and chaos, upheaval, desolation and discouragement, as well as a great deal of confusion.

People are often frightened and they do not know which way to turn, so I ask you to turn to each other and to turn within. Love is courageous, love is brave, love is stalwart and strong in the gentlest sense of the word.

When you have the fortitude to truly love yourself; every part, every fiber, every shadow, every cell, every element, all of your design; when you have the courage to admit that you are divinity in form, then you have the courage to go forward amidst the chaos. You also have the knowing that you do not do so alone, for in that divinity of self is a connectedness to All.

Many of you are experiencing exhaustion, physical and emotional trauma, pain, setbacks, and challenges. Many of you say you're fed up fed up and lonely. In some ways you feel broken, defeated and aban-doned. My friends, I know exactly how you feel, not merely through empathy or compassion, but through my very own human experience.

It is all right to feel this. You do not hurt our feelings. You do not anger the Mother/Father/One. You do not offend me. Don't deny any part of yourself, because when you do, it simply stops the flow of the energy. You wish this energy to flow quickly and smoothly away from you for it to be healed and gone.

You ask, "Lord, how does this get healed?" By loving yourself. By loving those emotions. I do not mean to stay with them, but to simply love them, then let them go.

If you saw a beautiful swan riding the current of the river, would you stop and enjoy the view and say, "There goes grace," or would you disturb the tableau and interfere? Let it go, dear ones, and then turn to me and accept the healing from myself and our Mother.

Bring us into your heart. Let us surround you. Many of you are ignoring your own personal guides and guardian angels. They can help you - that is their job, that is their commitment to One, that is their joy.

It always returns to this: Do you have the courage to love? Do you have the courage to go forward and be the pathfinder? Do you have the courage to walk with me to the places of love and victory? Do you have the courage to start again? I will show you how;

I will take your hand and walk with you.

During this time of rapid shifting in every layer and every sphere, you will get caught in the whirlpool if you do not consciously choose three things:

1) Love: Love of self and therefore love of All, and that includes every being, every plant, animal, fly, and human on the planet.

2) Joy: The joy of being alive. It is not just some momentary joy, "This will make me feel happy." It is the essential joy that you have chosen your divine form and are expressing it.

3) Courage: Knowing that sometimes, my beloved friends, courage means reaching out your hand to say, "Help, I am drowning."

We are with you. We keep saying this. We are with you as never before—we are next to you, we are in front of you, we are behind you. Let us help. Let us help this transformation and let us help you anchor this wondrous Nova Earth.

Do not forget your prayers and meditations for peace. They are more important than ever. Go with our love and go with my blessings. Take my hand and walk with me.

I Give You Peace

Welcome, brothers and sisters of my soul, I bring you peace. Do not concern yourself, my friends, by the seeming upheaval of political events in your country or by the changes being wrought all over this world—our planet of love.

I have told you this is the time of unfoldment of the Mother. Many atrocities have and will be revealed. These atrocities will be revealed for what they are: acts of deception, cruelty, greed and lust. I ask you to celebrate these revelations because these types of acts are being eliminated. They are being revealed that they may be cleared, and that the light and love of the day, the sun, and the Almighty Ones may shine on Earth and through the hearts of these beings.

My friends, this is not a time of judgment. It is a time to let go of all judgment within your beings and heart. It is a time, right here this day, to eliminate fear and greed, for there is no place on Nova Earth for such emotions.

The actions of hatred are ancient. It is no different than the Pharisees hating me, or the rabbis disdaining me because I was not of their club. The time of death, suffering, crucifixion and torture must come to an end, and it comes to an end with enlightened, gentle benevolence in your hearts.

None of you would tolerate the torture of a small child or of an animal. There are many forms of torture, but now the torture of each other comes to an end. If none forgives, if you do not find compassion in your heart and embrace each other as brothers and sisters, then there is no Nova Earth. And you know this is not the case.

You come together to not only create, but to manifest in physicality a new planet of love. I am so excited to witness this and to be with you to do this, to walk with you and to celebrate with you, to share our victory and to turn to the Mother and say, "We have completed, and we have begun."

Allow this to begin. Open your hearts and be the leaders of this nation. Forgive and accept the role each plays in this unfoldment.

Give thanks and know I am with you each and every moment of your life.

The Gift of Mercy

I come to speak to you of mercy, of this beautiful quality which is so needed during this unfoldment. I also say it has always been needed, and it has always been a blessing and a gift. But from time to time my friends there are needs for reminders. I wish to talk to you about mercy because there is need for mercy, and you, my bright angels have the capacity, wisdom, heart and love to truly know, express and practice mercy.

Think of mercy in this way: it is compassion+forgiveness+love. Mercy is not merely the ability or the action, the heart knowing of forgiveness; it is a component. Similarly, it is not just compassion; it is not merely being the observer of the other person or persons' position. And it is not just love, although love is all, but I speak of love in

this regard also as an action, an expression, and an experience.

There are occurrences, personal and collective tragedies such as mass slaughter, that carry the energy of overwhelm and in that, conscious and unconscious, of lack of power, of feeling powerless and of feeling the sense of collective guilt and shame that such things could happen. In that there is almost an autonomic reflex to attempt to distance yourself, because it is so atrocious that you want to extend it away from your being.

Mercy has the same magnitude as overwhelm and it encompasses all of these feelings. It encompasses and embraces everyone involved; those who have died, those who have expired, those who have been injured, those that have been present, the families, the extended families, the community, the perpetrator—his family or her family—their community, the media and the police.

To be merciful is one of the deepest senses of being the observer, quasi-participant. Let me explain: When you hold and give at the same time, because mercy only becomes the fullness of its quality—of this element of mercy—when it is extended, when it is put into the flow. That does not mean intervention. That does not mean that you involve yourself, that is why I say quasi-participant, but you observe, you observe these situations.

In tragic situations, be they personal or collective, they are tragic because everyone suffers, no one is exempt. Hence it is important that you remain the observer, embracing the entire situation because all involved call out for mercy—the forgiveness, compassion, and love, which is the healing. You enfold them gently in this quality of mercy that they will be comforted. In that giving of comfort and mercy, you are also given comfort and mercy. You receive exactly and more than what you give.

Often in your dramas, real and manufactured, people will plead for mercy, which is different than clemency. Mercy is that forgiveness, it is the understanding of compassion, and it is the love to see that bright spark, the original soul design of everyone involved.

Now, fortunately, you have not been engaged recently, actively, in these tragedies and yes, I ask you to send the mercy and enfold the planet and everyone who needs this. But I also ask you, my family, to extend this mercy to yourself. So often you will say, "Well, I forgive myself; I have compassion for myself; oh, I love myself." Expand it, combine it, and give yourself my tender mercy. Let me comfort you that you may comfort others. This is the gift of my heart to you, to each of you this day. I love you deeply.

Trust & Forgiveness

I wish to speak to you of trust and forgiveness. The keys to heaven are trust and forgiveness, love, unity, connectedness and balance.

You have integrated many aspects, expanded the core of your being and brought it into alignment with your divine sacred self, with the perfection of who you are. This is wondrous for us to gaze upon. Even when you are uncertain, you are in beauty and grace.

During these times of great change upon the planet and within your heart, it is important, my friends, to trust yourself as you have never trusted before. You can do this from your sense of expanded self, from the wisdom in knowing not only who you are, but where you are within the greater unfoldment. The key is to not look outside of yourself for the nod of approval or acceptance. Particularly, do not look to the conventional signposts, but rather, dear one, look within your heart. Look deep within and into that place of love. Trust yourself to know which actions to take and how to proceed, to know what is truth and what is illusion.

I have told you that much illusion would be revealed; now you can begin to see what I have been speaking of. There will be much turmoil and upheaval, and it is all a part of this process of the unfoldment of the Mother and Her love upon the Earth. Trust those who touch your heart in love. Forgive those who come to you in judgment, in harshness. Forgive those you previously would have judged as right or wrong, loving or not. Understand they are simply in the struggle of accepting their own divinity and releasing the old beliefs of who they are.

There is a saying and an understanding that institutions take on a life of their own, but let us be clear—institutions and bureaucracies either stand in truth or not; it is that simple. Do not worry about the "if and how" institutions will transform or crumble. Simply reach out to each being that is affected, each brother and sister, because that is what they are—a person exactly the same as you, a mirror of your being discovering their own love and heart. They will need to be forgiven and embraced.

This unfoldment is not about exclusion. It is about throwing open your arms and welcoming home those who have been lost. Yes, the parable that I told long ago about the lost lamb still holds true and it is does not matter whether it is a child, an army private or a president; be clear on this. Have compassion, take these feelings of disdain and separation and throw them away. When you are horrified do not point your finger. Feel the sadness and release it, understanding the unity and the connection of all. It is not your brother or sister that has fallen into chaos; it is the collective; it is you and I. By holding our center, by holding the light,

we heal and transform; we transmute the pain.

You have gone through processes in the past-while of being reborn. Share this knowing, understanding that there are times when being reborn feels much more difficult than dying. You have gone through your traumas, your dramas and the throes of reinvention from this place of knowing and understanding. Give compassion; send compassion to those who follow you, for you are the pathfinders. You are the showers of the way. You are bringing them to light.

Show others how to be reborn; how to walk through the passageway of the 13th Octave, to the reception corridor where Archangels Gabrielle and Michael await. You do this in love and gentleness. Understand that this process is helpful for many in transition or fighting the wages of war. This is not about a physical death, but rather for them to be escorted, met by their own circle of guides and friends, this Council, and their own sweet self. They will not go off with us; they will return back down that spiraled corridor of light, hand in hand with you, knowing that you have been connected and reconnected in love. Make this your peace meditation and look for me, my brothers, my sisters, my family—for I will be there too. Go with my love.

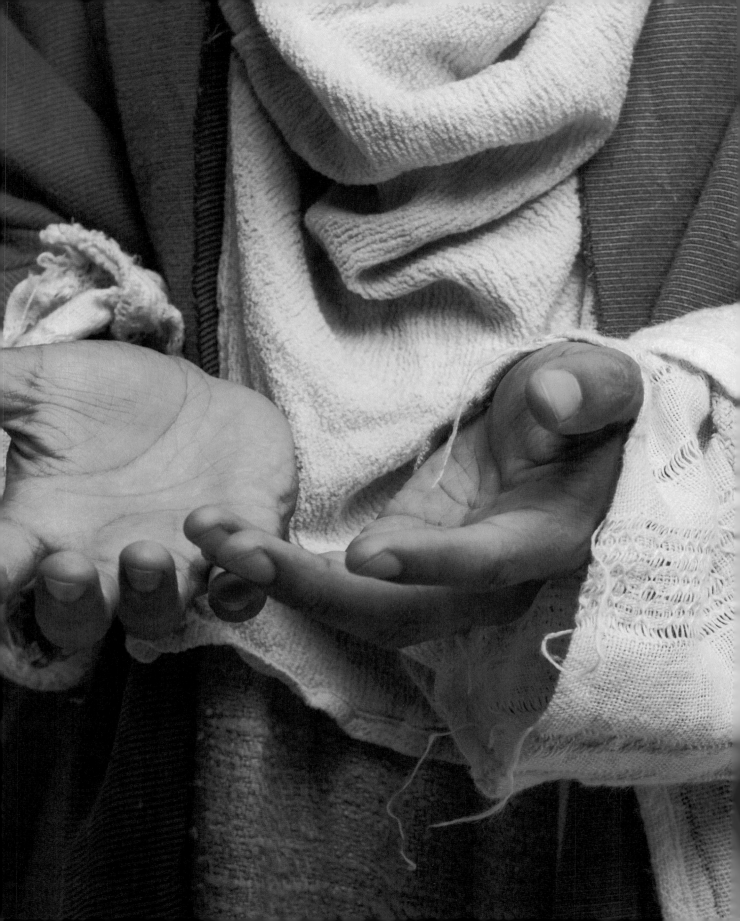

CHAPTER 7
HEALING &
CREATION

So many times you've asked, "Jesus, how can we teach of love when there are the poor and hungry, and those who are in pain and who suffer with their physical ailments? Teach us first how to heal and how to feed our families."

The Role of Healer

When I walked the Earth there were times when there wasn't enough, but we did not feel poor. We shared our resources; we shared our food and our homes. We went together to visit the sick and dying. Always I would ask, "Do you think this person wishes to continue as part of our tribe, or do you think they wish to go home to the Father and feast at His banquet table?"

I would get replies such as, "Oh, this one wishes to live, for though she is old, she is expecting her first born." or, "Although she is paralyzed, her spirit is strong." I would speak to the heart and soul of each being whom I healed. When they said, "Yes," the healing was instantaneous. When they said, "No," it was swift passage home.

We would help them to clear their hearts, to take care of the affairs of their family in order that they could live or leave in peace. There is no death; there is only life. Each of you has lived many times and you know the cycle of rebirth. Each of you has chosen to return to Earth again and again to bring the promise of love.

Every time you return to the Mother's arms, you say, "That's it, never again." Believe me, I've done the same. She looks at you and She speaks of Her mission of love, of Her angels in form. She speaks of a world where there is no suffering and disease, where the garden is restored, and always you say, "Oh, alright; I will help with that." This is the lifetime of fulfillment, my friends.

When I walked the Earth I did not claim special powers as healer. What I claimed was the privilege and honor of the alignment with the Holy Spirit, with the Mother and Father. When I allowed that to flow through me, it did not matter whether the person was dead and buried or many miles away, they were healed. Not because of Jesus the man, but because I, the man, stepped aside.

The many angels and masters of healing who come to join you do not say, "Use my power." They offer to help and to be of service. Even when they say, "Let me in," know that they're gently nudging you aside a little bit so the energy can flow. Allow them to do this; truly they only come in gentleness, to assist you in your chosen mission.

So what is the role of the healer? Often, I have said to you, "Each one of you is healer and teacher." You turned to me and laughed and said, "But I am a nurse, I am a chemist, I am a farmer." Yes, you are. You also are a healer and a teacher.

There are many professions in this wondrous world where what you do is holy and sacred. I'm not asking you to replace your chosen path, as it is the way in which you approach it that matters.

When I was on Earth, I said, "Love your neighbor as yourself." Again, I ask you to love yourself as you love your neighbor. Each one of you needs to expand the wellspring of your deep regard for your beloved self. Inside that deep regard is the recognition of yourself as healer and teacher, as nurturer, that's all there is. It is the gentle showing; it is being the mirror of God, so the other person can look into your eyes and say, "There I am."

Healing is instantaneous. But the heart, mind, and body of the human race is very slow, even as your world has sped up. You do not create the time to sit, listen, heal, to touch the Earth and touch the sky. Part of your role as a healer is to help people take this time. It is particularly effective if a person receiving healing is lying down, for then they feel that you are directing it and they will stay put.

Even in your busyness, rather than speaking to someone on the fly, make sure you take the time to say, "Sit with me for a moment." It is not the subject at hand that is important; it is not about giving and receiving information and instruction. It is about saying, "You are important enough in my eyes, and the eyes of God, to be with for a moment. Let me show you how dear you are."

The Mission of Healing

When I walked the world before, there were not so many people or so much disarray. The Earth had not suffered so much, even after eons of existence. But now is a time of healing of the Earth and humanity; the hearts and souls of many.

Many are required to assist in this task, and many have stepped forward. They and you are part of the Legion of the Mother, and it is this Legion which has come together to heal. We do not care what your politics are; it is the politics of peace, which will heal every fiber of the planet. You simply remain in your heart.

I walk with you and I heal with you; know this. We are joined in heart, purpose and mission, never to be separated, together as one. Go forward fearlessly as you have been taught and reminded. Call upon your gifts and use them wisely: share them, give them, and celebrate them.

I give you my heart. Walk softly and never worry about technicalities, for regimes come and go. Rome, Egypt, Babylonia, Syria—even the New Jerusalem—will one day be dust.

The Offer of Healing

I have spoken to you so many times about the love I have for you. The honor and respect never diminishes, it just grows.

As you go forward in this shifting, not only of Earth, but the frequency of the collective, know that life is not always easy. Hence, I want you know that I am here, not only as brother and friend, but healer as well.

If you were to actively engage in a program, whether it was an isolation chamber or an anti-gravity chamber; or if you were preparing to fly to Mars, then you would feel what it is like being in a very different energy field. Because of that, you would have different physical reactions. Although it is not being publicly announced, and is not being calibrated in ways that your scientists understand, many of your scientific and technical communities are noticing that the patterns of the movement of energy are shifting. This will not be kept secret indefinitely, because it is the scientific community and particularly the physicists that love to play with these changes.

Call on me if you are not feeling perfect in your heart, your head, or your physical body, for there are legions of us here to help. We do not wish to slow down this process of shift, and neither do you. But we can certainly help temper it and help your body adjust to these frequencies. There are many of us working strictly on this at this time.

I walk this planet with you in this moment as part of you, as you are part of me that I may heal you, for my ministry was always one of healing and compassion. There is need for many hands and many brave souls; a task for the most courageous.

The demons that you face are your own. They are to be conquered, embraced and loved, for they show you the pathways to the hearts of your brothers and sisters. So, call them forth that they will confront you. Embrace them that they may become their radiant selves with you. It is time for integration of all aspects into one form, the form you have chosen.

Turn to us and call our name, call my name, whisper my name. Ask for help; that is our joy, my joy, our service to the Mother, and beloveds to each of you. You do not need to understand how this healing works. Understand, it is the transmission of divine radiance directly into your physicality. It is the transmission of love to your very cells, organs and entirety. Sweet angels of light do not hesitate to call us.

Understanding The Grid

I come this day to speak to you of healing, and of the Golden Grid. It is named after Archangel Gabrielle and is electromagnetic in its energy and nature. I speak about the grid so you will understand it in relationship to your healing work. Understand, we have all begun as One; as one entity, one heart, and one essence of connection.

As each of you began to venture forth, you were given a highway of energy grids to travel upon. You were given substance and form, and this was known as your grid. This grid was cast wide that none would ever be disconnected or lost; at all levels you would know that you were intimately connected to all. There would be no illusion of separation; there would be no belief in distance.

What happened, as a matter of choice and memory, is that you, humanity, adopted illusions of separation, but the grid never disappeared. Upon the Earth, the grid became frayed and tattered. It has been greatly abused by those upon the planet, by many who were of greed and lust, hatred and war. But never was the etheric blueprint lost; never was the patterning destroyed; that is not permitted.

In 2001, the Earth grid was restored and reconnected with the universal grid that you have always been part of and which has been intact for a very, very long time – what you tend to think of as eons. It has been restored that you may be reunited with your universal brothers and sisters—not only upon the planet of Earth, but throughout the cosmos—that you will begin to remember, through the movement of energy through your being, that you are interconnected with all.

The blue diamonds of the Mother are the seeds of reawakening; the seeds of consciousness that have been planted and replanted within you so you may blossom in your wholeness upon this grid. There are many upon the planet that still cling to the old grids of illusion, even though underneath it, the Earth grid has been restored. With humanity, it is not that we are trying

to restore or replace personal grids. They are already present and perfect. Many of you don't see that, simply because you have covered it up—much the same as you cover your bodies with clothes. You cover yourself with layers of false grids of illusion and destruction, limitation, lack and disease.

Your role as a healer is to help remove these grids of false beliefs and activate the true grid that was originally implanted. You help the individual and the collective to become one again, and be comfortable with that reality. Then the joy of being connected in heart, and heart to heart will be known.

The plan of restoration of love upon the planet, of the healing of the hearts of humanity, is not simply for the planet; it is for this and many universes. For when there is one hole or tatter in the grid, all suffer. It is this restoration that you have volunteered for; that is what your Mother asks you to step forward to do.

Each of you does this in very different ways; that is the diversity that each of you has chosen. It is the luxury of this experience; it is the joy. We repeat to you; do not change who you are. You are perfect. You always have been; you simply need to remember that, to look in the mirror and love yourself.

As I walk this planet, I see much devastation, much need for repair work. So do not limit yourself simply to one place, one time or one person or group. Send your essence forward out into your world to complete the healing that needs to take place. You have full capacity to be in many places at once. It is something that you were born with; it is something that you have always had. When I speak of being born, I mean the moment that you emanated from the heart of One.

Join with me in this healing of Earth. Join me in the Middle East, on the plains of Africa, in your inner cities, and in your places of stillness and calm. You are positioned in your part of the world to temper the energies, to hold your own and Earth's grid intact with any shifts in the electromagnetic fields.

I do not mean that there will be unmanageable chaos and mass destruction, for that is not of love, charity or prudence. Chaos does not reflect divine intention. There are many above you who watch over you patiently and guide you in these transitions.

It is the time of rebirth of the idea, belief, and knowing of what humanity truly is. It is not an idea that has ever changed, in my heart or yours. It is a belief, idea and action; the knowing and will of love.

The expansion of your being is not simply your hearts. I come this day, in love, to ask you to realign your entire being; for all parts of you—every aspect, every hair, every lifetime—was and is not only necessary, but desirable and celebrated.

The Plan of the Mother is for alignment directly with Her Heart, Will and Mind. It is the unity of Trinity; it is the union of All.

You say, "Yes, Jesus, but when will I know that I am in alignment with the Divine Mind, and when will I know if it is ego?"

You have scales of justice and truth which rest within your heart. Those scales within your heart are your balancer. When you look at your intelligence, at what you create with mind, your theories that take form and matter, balance them within you and see if they are of love. Do the same with your actions and with your will—for it is your will that puts both of these into form on the planet and throughout the universe. When your will is out of alignment with All, simply step aside and place yourself upon your golden grid and allow the energy, that current of love, to flow. Do not force this alignment; it will come naturally, as naturally as sunrise and sunset, and you will find yourself once again in harmony. It is when you try to force and hold the belief that you are separate from this grid of All, that trouble ensues.

It is very, very simple. What you are doing is simply balancing your grid. It is everything. It is the framework upon which reality rests.

When you are lonely, reach out your hand upon this grid and feel my touch and energy as I send you love. Feel my peace and allow it to flow through you, to your neighbors, and family, and to your planet.

The electromagnetic grid is fueled by love. It is the unseen force that creates from the stillpoint of nothingness. It is the fuel of the universe, be it at rest or in movement, it is exactly the same.

The stillpoint of your heart is your ground zero; it is that simple. We do not urge you to go scurrying around the planet looking for your point of zero; consider it to be Earth—for you are that large, my brothers and sisters. You are the earth; you carry it within you and outside of you—that is the Universal Law. It is reflected both ways.

The Current of Love

My message to you today is about the power of love. Love is the essence, the heart, the mind and the will of One. It does not need to be created as it is the essence of All, but it does need to be activated and placed inside of each and every heart. When you are healing, that is the switch you are turning on in yourself or another. It is the current, the electricity, of love. It is the energy of One.

When there is difficulty in your grid, which is part of the golden grid that unites all, there is a blockage either in the cells of your body, the skeleton of your being, or the golden lines of energy connecting you to the heart of One. A blockage means that the current of love has either been turned off or turned down so low that it is no longer felt. To remedy this, both as a healer and a human, you need to turn on the switch, the love energy flow again. That is what healing and grid work is about; it is making sure

the current of love is flowing in its golden radiance everywhere, freely and openly.

At any given moment in time you are able to sit still and feel this flow of energy. When you go to the stillpoint of your being, take in a deep breath, and out of that breath of stored-up energy, create something new, and let it explode along the grid. It is the most fun that any being can have, in any universe. I invite you to play with it.

To come to earth and witness sickness, death and dying, pain and suffering is tedious. Each one of you has said that again and again. I agree. Let us change it together. Let us join our hearts together again; let us join in victory and heal all dis-ease.

When you return home again to the Mother and say, "Never again." She will accept your answer. But you will come back; you will come back again to witness the beauty that you are creating this and every day.

Do not doubt your power to heal yourself, each other and this beautiful planet. If you feel that you are having trouble turning on the switch to your own current or to anyone else's, call on me. I am a master electrician, not just carpenter; I will throw the switch with you and for you.

Empathy & Protection

There are so many upon this planet who think it a blessing and a curse to know the

169

heart, mind and inner workings of another. Most who have now returned to the Earth are empathic and have a strong connection to the heart of One, a bond that can never be severed. You have a knowing connection to each being, heart and each expression of individuality throughout the universe. Do not shut it off or turn away from it.

To be empathic does not mean you need to assume the heart, feelings and experiences of another. To know and acknowledge is one thing; to stand back and be the observer is what you need to do. Do you not think, as I stood before Pontius Pilate, that I didn't know his heart, as my fellow Jews cursed me? That I didn't know, as my brothers and apostles ran away, their feelings and thoughts?

I knew them as I know each of your hearts. I don't invade your privacy, but often you reach out to me, as I do to you. I do not take your feelings from you, unless you have asked and you completed what you need to experience. Do not simply release and keep going; grow and find the joy that is underneath.

When you are empathic, and you believe that this means you need to assume another's feelings—you are wrong. It is incorrect direction. Look at it, honor it; send your love and very often your mercy, compassion and healing. Touch and open their hearts, but do not steal their goods.

Let us be clear that there is a difference as well, between empathy and protection. I have talked of this, and do so again. There is great need, during this time of chaos, for each one of you to protect your sacred space, your beautiful beings. Do not absorb unconsciously or unwittingly the very energy of turmoil that is in the air.

The intensity of release, which is the good news, is such that you need protection. We ask of you as well to seal your space, homes, places of work and communities with the archangels and with the Trinity. In doing this, you will ensure that there are no trespassers allowed. You stay within your space as you move about and do your sacred work.

Seal your space as you go among the masses to do your work. This is not a time to say, "It is chaotic out there and I will stay home." It is a time to tend to those who have yearning to go forward, who yearn to know love. There are many upon your planet who do not wish to live, who are welcomed back home into the light to complete their journeys in the heart of One. That is the expression and freedom; it is never judged. Do not impede those who wish to return to us, but to those who wish to remain, give the full force of your healing, teaching and messages. Open your empathic channel that you will know how to touch the world and open their hearts. Help them heal themselves.

The Gift of Stillness

You are given many gifts to go forward and heal this planet, and teach the words of love, compassion and forgiveness.

Your planet is in a time of transition and the process of reawakening. It is the Mother's Plan that you release your attachments to certain patterns of behavior which do not serve you or anyone else. These are coming to the forefront fast and furious. You have very dramatic examples of this in the government of nations, as well as up close and personal examples each and every day.

Understand that you have stood in judgment—have had positive or negative, good or bad opinions about people in turmoil—but the truth is that it simply is. It does not matter whether it is the excitement of war or the excitement of peace; you need to stay in the place of calm detachment and observation, because this is the place you conduct your work from. This does not mean you are not simultaneously fully connected to All, and to the absence of all.

The ability to stay in the place of calm and non-attachment is crucial to multi-location, of being in existence throughout the universe. When you become involved in the energy field and the drama of another being, you are not fully anchored within your own heart. Remember it is from the place of anchoring within your heart, that you send the love, recognition and blessings. It is also the place where the core of your being rests in absolute centeredness and grounding.

When you are in the whirlwind of another's energy field, you are not grounded in your own, and you lose the greatest percentage of the effectiveness you have to offer. Hence, the teaching, healing and channeling does not occur with the same level of intensity or genuine love.

It is not your role, and it is not the role of any being, no master or saint, to assume the energy of another; that is not for the highest good of any. When we say to you, "Give us your fear, give us your anger, give us your frustration," we do not take it from you and store it in our bellies. We take it and, like the dove, we set it free. We return it to One, transmuting it instantaneously back to light. That is what you need to do. That is the gift that you give to humanity. It is a gift of healing, of transformation and transmutation of energy of all kinds.

Many of you have been the teachers of the small ones, of the children. You have talked and laughed about sometimes how they bounce off ceilings and walls. As a teacher you do not go into the room and say, "Calm down or I will bounce you off the walls." That is not how you proceed. You calm the energy, you open their hearts and minds to enthusiasm, and then you proceed.

That is what you do with the populace of Earth. You calm them, you heal them, and then you say, "Let us discover this universe of unlimited potential together. I will show you how. I will teach you how to read the stars of heaven. I will show you the symbols and the messages of the universe that you can read, know and understand how things work, and who you are, and why you walk this planet."

That is the gift of teachers. The gift of healing is the gift of stillness, of allowing the energy to flow through you to the heart of the person, that they, in their own quiet place, can open to the love, and to the love of themselves. In the stillness, you assist so that they can release the pain they carry. The healer is always the teacher. The healing is never complete unless you have given the gift of understanding of how they can do this themselves.

There is no reality in which codependency is a virtue. My friends, not only are you working miracles—you are a miracle! It is a miracle that you stand and sit on this Earth. You have chosen to be the strong ones, to be the vessels of physical manifestation. That is why so many of us return as well—not simply to return as your teachers and healers, but as your fellow journeymen. We return because it is a gift of unconditional love to help manifest the Mother's Plan in physical form, to anchor the consciousness of love in physical form.

Do not underestimate your power to create. You have done mighty work already and you have just begun. You are given the gift of spontaneous creation; it is creation born of the joining of essence and the union of heart, love and dreams. To be in physical form does not mean that you are not to dream, for it is in the grand dreaming and the wishes of what you can create upon this planet, that the miracles will multiply. You have known this forever.

You are a personal choice and expression of God, of the One unity of love, just like air and water. Air and water are the most unimpeded sources of life upon Earth; they are sources of love. Water and air are two of the many ways in which God's force moves through you. They are essential commodities of this planet and gifts from the One.

Each one of you will find yourself more and more drawn to air, light and water. It is not coincidence that I transmuted water into wine; it is the life's blood of this planet, and it is the life's blood of One.

Healing & Creation

It is not the awakening of your power to create and heal, but the remembering that you may do so. There has been much creation on this planet since first I walked, and yet there are still the illusions that now need to die, so that new life may live.

Healing is but a form, an expression, of creation. I have told you many times that healing occurs instantaneously. However, most people do not believe or understand that they are worthy of this instantaneous

healing and therefore one takes time for healing another, regardless of the approach or modality. You do so out of compassion for your brothers and sisters who are wounded in heart. You take the time to listen, touch and nurture. Truly what you are doing is saying, "You are worth it." This has been the key issue for humanity for many, many years; it is the recognition of self-worth in one's self and each other.

Many of you have witnessed abuse of power; you have abused power, and have been abused by power, and so the pendulum goes. However, it is time to finish this cycle and begin anew. It is human grace that creates. You will be assisted by many, above and below, but the creation and fulfillment of the dream of Nova Earth is yours. That is why you are here; not simply to witness mayhem, but to create anew. Go into your heart and begin this day to choose grace, and the new; for that is truly what this life is about.

Your Ability to Create

I do not walk this beautiful garden of Gaia, as you do at this time. But I have walked, and I have walked with many of you. I know what it is to be a man, and to have the worries and concerns of family, of friends, of politics. I wish to speak to you from this perspective.

My beloved ones, as a child, I was very clear about my mission and purpose on Earth. Either in body form or not, that has never changed. My purpose is to teach and be love. It sounds so simple, and it is, because it is the essence, it is the core of who you and I are. You don't need to seek divinity, you don't need to seek love - it is already imbedded deep within your core.

But what happens in our human journey is you allow fear and worry and things that are really insignificant to creep in. There is no need to. You ask, "Well, how do I stop it? I'm not sure if I can pay my mortgage or my rent. I'm not sure if I can feed my family." I know these feelings because I was a poor carpenter. I did not earn a lot of money, but I did believe in miracles. I believed in the power of creation that I held within me; not as Son of God, but as man.

The trust, hope, and knowing I could bring forth what was required physically was a given. I practiced it, again, and again, and again. I didn't allow other's fears to distract me. I knew my sacred contract as man with Father/Mother/One assured me that I was attended and tended to, that I was loved; just as you are loved.

You have the ability to create what your heart desires. You have the ability to eliminate the chaos from you and your family's life. Let me teach you how. Come with me and come with this Council. Allow me to show you how to work the creation formula; how to practice it in your daily life; how to anchor your dearest heart's desires.

The Building Block of Creation is Love

There has been much discussion about creation. I want to talk to you about love in the context of creation. When I walked the Earth, love was my soul design. It was my soul purpose and my creation and co-creation with my family, my friends, and with each of you.

Love is the fundamental building block of anything you want to create. If you do not have love, if you do not have joy, if you do not have that sense of self, then you cannot have a sense outside of yourself.

What has always endured is love. You are not "about" to become whole. You are not "about" to become masters. You are not "about" to become divine. You already are! That's not ego; that is the acceptance that you are born from the seed, heart and womb of the universe, of the Mother/Father/God/One, and you are born of love. The collection of your molecules, your matter—from your toes to your hair, to your expanded field, to your inner force field—it is all love.

Long ago, some would ask, "Jesus, do you not have anything to talk about other than love? What about the law and the traditions?" I'd shake my head no. As you well know, it is not that I was not steeped in the traditions and the law, but that was not what was important.

What is important, what people need to remember is the union between brothers, friends and enemies needs to be love; then there is no conflict. Of course, there are healthy differences of opinion—this is the planet of diversity; it was the way it was created and part of the delight.

But my message has never changed. As you step forward in this unity of creation, you are recognizing, allowing, surrendering and embracing the love of who you are, and in that, the love of each other and the love of all things. It has never been a hierarchy.

Don't think because I don't walk on Earth in physical form, that I am not still creating. I am constantly creating, as are you. The areas where I choose to create, where I choose to place my energies, are those that create unity of heart and unity of purpose.

I honor your creations; many of them are heartening, fun and playful. I will assist you, adding my energy to yours in what your heart desires, but I ask you to do the same; I ask you, as co-creators on this planet in form, to add your energy to mine to create love in form, in action, in community on this wondrous planet that our Mother has given us.

You are capable of this. You always have been. It is simply a matter of acknowledging what you are doing here, claiming your birthright and stepping fully into who you really are. The Mother has ignited your divinity, but it is you my beloved ones, who

live it, exhibit it and share it. Do this with me—that is my request; that is my prayer. Come create with me.

Creating Change

My beloved friends, you have been given the gift of the 13th Octave, the most precious gift of completion and of All. This is the love, and the state of being in the unity of One, in the unity of home. Often when I walked the Earth, many turned to me and asked me why things did not seem to bother me. Quite frankly, it is not that they did not bother me; I was good at not showing it. Yet, in truth, they did not bother me because I knew there was no separation. For as man, not a master, I was connected to my Mother/Father/One. When you are in this place of unity, that is true for you as well. All is possible.

I come to talk about the potential for human experience in its totality. We have talked to you about the potential to heal, create, teach and unify. It is this potential within your physical form that is the true intention and plan of who you are. This is not a new discovery; this is a return to the plan for the human race: to be angelic, universal beings of mastery, having an experience of being physical.

The illusions and the veil have become denser and denser until you have truly believed that what is happening within your field—inside that bubble as it were—is reality. It is only a small portion of what is available to all of you.

So often you have turned to me and asked, 'Lord, we accept and know we are pathfinders and showers of the way, Nova Beings; but how on Earth are we going to create these changes by the completion of this cycle? How will we do this? How will we break through?"

My friends, you do it by drawing upon all that is available to you, not only from this realm, but from the realm of your reality of Earth. What is required to create change is a fundamental understanding of how to manage and manipulate change. What is required to heal hatred is love, and so on.

You are breaking free to simply gather within this Earth realm what has always been available to you—and then we will teach you how to reach beyond. This is the beginning my friends, not the end. Go with my love, go with my help. You are cherished.

CHAPTER 8
NOVA EARTH

This is a time of extraordinary change. Welcome to today and the future. But before I proceed, let's reflect back on the past.

Sweet angels of light, you have done stalwart work. Has it been a year where you have practiced and become more patient, wise, compassionate and understanding? You have become more deeply in love with us, the universe, each other, and most importantly, with your sacred self.

Times of Extraordinary Change

The Mother has spoken, taught, and demonstrated a great deal about sacred union and the true meaning of sacred union within and without. Without the deepening of this love affair with your sacred self, all of Her words have no meaning.

This is not what has occurred—for you have accepted, indeed grabbed and integrated all the energetic downloads that have been sent to you. You have welcomed the shift, the change, and the deepest levels of integration. Even as you've readied, you have asked, "Lord, what next?" Well, hold on to your hats, hold on to your socks, and unfurl your wings!

You have come to this beloved planet of Gaia initially as masters-in-the-making, but you have claimed and stepped forward, allowed, accepted and surrendered to your mastery. So now you wonder, "What's next; where are we going?"

You have challenged and cleared many of your core issues; enough that you have the essence of clarity needed to proceed. It is no longer sufficient, acceptable, and certainly not fun to be limited, shackled, and jailed in what remains of the old third dimension.

So on to the next chapter of your journey of wholeness. For this new time is the intertwining, the integration of all. That is why, when I have spoken of who I am, I speak of the seventh dimension—the dimension of love—the halfway point between the first dimensions and the higher dimensions, or what you tend to think of as the higher dimensions. The seventh dimension is the home of love, but it is also the point, the state of being, of integration.

So often we speak of love; that is the truth, essence, microcosm and macrocosm of the entire universe. It is the essence of our beloved Mother and Father. It is the integrated source of All.

But, what is love? Often we have said, "It is peace, serenity, bliss, ecstasy, knowing, and wisdom." How you come to know love is through experiential existence. It doesn't matter whether it is in the first or the twelfth dimension. How you experience love is how you know it.

You tend to think of the Father as "the great silence," the Unknowable Source; He is love. The Mother is "the movement," "the nurturer," the Creator Source; She is love. But it is an act of will, energy of will from the very core of Source—that activates and moves the Mother; it joins with the Mother into movement, creation, and action.

This is what is taking place within you right now. You are being activated to the deepest and highest integration of love and will. The expression of that divine union is action. It is the action of loving; being gentle, kind and nurturing to your beloved, divine, human and inter-multidimensional self. It is the expression and action of love in the external reality, with us and with all realms, including the angels, archangels, masters, and most importantly, with each other. The work that you have done brings you to this time and place where, by an act of loving will, you are prepared to move forth, right now, in action.

And what is the expression, the knowing, and the experience of this action? It is joy, it is bliss, and ultimately it is ecstasy. It is the integration of all of you, with all of humanity, and with the All. That is where you are headed in this year and this time.

There is some groundwork for this, such as clearing core issues, embracing joy, the acceptance of greater love and knowingness. You have reached a place of balance, of wisdom in knowing what creates balance. Where there is hatred, you balance it with compassion and love. Where there is dissonance, you bring clarity. Where there is inequality, you bring equality. Where

there is lack, you add abundance. You have learned this; you have learned it within, and now you move boldly, freely, in awe and excitement, into the creation and co-creation of Nova Earth, from the place of Nova Being and loving will.

Sometimes you ask, "Lord, when will we be free?" You have always been free! But, somehow you did not get the memo; you did not receive the text.

It is not a matter of more activation. It is not a matter of more tsunamis. You are the agents of extraordinary change. You are the agents and the angels of regridding, of repatterning and of pulling, pushing and gentling with every ounce of your being.

What this means in practical terms is—it is a world that you have not even yet seen. You have dreamt of the new tomorrow and you have believed it to be fabulous, and in fact it has been, but you aren't even close. It is not ten years hence or one hundred years hence; it is right now. And what does it look like, other than pristine, clean, balanced, trusting and loving? It looks like love in action, in play, in harmony, in silence, and in the sound of Archangel Gabrielle's horn calling all into attendance and balance. It looks and it feels like extraordinary movement.

Why do I use the term "extraordinary?" The understanding that change is constant, is universal. You will not be the same in the next breath that you were a moment ago. The Mother's creation is constant and infinite; therefore, change is constant and infinite. That is ordinary, which is really far from ordinary. I use this term "extraordinary" to connote quantum leaps; change of such a magnitude that you can hardly believe that yesterday was yesterday and today is today.

Now, what is required in all of this? Simple acceptance. I am asking you to walk with me, to walk with us, to walk on Earth with the masters, in form now! And I know you say, "Yes." Your heart, your soul, has always said, "Yes."

Expect the unexpected, revel in it. Ascension is at hand, and so take each other's hands, take my hand, take the hand of St. Germaine, Sanat Kumara, the Mother— because we proceed together in love, determination, and focused action.

What Lies Ahead

On Earth, there are many words that are overused. If I am to say to you, "Remarkable, incredible, magnificent transformation." You say, "Yeah, ok, I know that, but what else?"

What does magnificent transformation look like for Gaia, for this beloved planet? Gaia is spinning faster than ever. Earth has begun her transformation. The work you are doing and have done is not only for yourself, but also a deep reassurance to her. You have the expression that you are ready

for take off. Well, she, too, is ready for take off. You have done the preparation, you have made the flight. You reassure not only the human collective, you reassure Gaia she does not need to do any more shrugging. She does not need to give strong messages of, "Get ready." She has no desire to create devastation—cleansing, yes; devastation, no.

You have said to all of us, and for the human collective, "We are ready, we are there!" We have waited so long for your readiness.

This transformation is not about oceans overtaking land mass. There has been drift of the axis of about three degrees over the last twenty-five to thirty years. That shift affects what you tend to think of as changing weather patterns. The shift goes south by southwest; it is very marginal. That shift is not an axis or a pole shift; that will not take place. There are not times of darkness. There are not times of shortages. Your electrical grids will be recharged. This transformation is about unity, about building a community of love.

St. Germaine, my dear friend and physician, used to tease you and call you M & M's—"Masters-in-the-Making." Now you are simply in your mastery. The only thing that bars you from this is your own sense of self-acceptance. We are pleased there is also enough ego to accept it. Do not deny who you are, for it belittles us.

I walk with you and we break bread together. All of this is important as a part of maintaining balance as you go about your work. The issue of balance is one of eternal concern, for you can no longer have a person or a planet out of balance. That is not the Divine Plan.

Take time for your sacred self. Take time to listen, to create, to be who you are. The changes are rapid and your physical form is becoming stronger and stronger. That does not mean that we are asking you to be triathletes. We are asking you to be in the balance. That means rest, that means play, that means honoring what you need. Not next week, not when you can fit it in. You can say, "Well, you know, I'll get to that next week." It doesn't work that way. The time is now.

You have entered a dimensional reality where time is very different, my friends. I would suggest you adjust your watches. (You can toss them, unless you like the jewelry.) You are already walking in the Cities of Light. You carry this transformation within you, but you are also there. You are spanning not only a year, but a very big archway, a bridge of time: a bridge to tomorrow, and a bridge to now.

What Is The Mother's New Time

Time is part of your definition of the human experience. In the past year, the Mother has declared Her New Time, but let us first talk about your mental, emotional, and physical construct of time—both as it has been and as it is shifting. Many of you have felt this interdimensional slippage, this time slippage—and this is a good thing. It is one of those signs many have been waiting and looking for.

When you enter into the realm of physicality on Earth, you are given time in order to be able to anchor within the expanse of space length and width, of emotionality and mental constructs, etc.

You may think of zero to ninety of your years as being within the brackets that the Mother inserts for the experience of your time and most people's time upon this planet. At one end of those brackets is infinity or the infinite, and at the other end is eternity or the eternal. Those brackets have been perceived as solid, and within them you have the somewhat linear experience of time. That perception of solidity is why you age and have the experience of being one, two, twenty, and ninety. That is one of the ways in which you experience being in form on Earth. It is the construct in which you came to express and share what it is like to be in form as sacred divine beings. It is your experience of love in form.

It is simple. The Mother says, "How do you want to experience love in form?" You say, "I want to go to Earth and see what that's like." And she says to you, "Oh good, because I have a huge project down there. What I'm doing is reanchoring the original Plan for Gaia and the Father and I want love. We want this planet to be an entire planet of love. We want physical reality of sacred union and partnership. We want physical reality of the expression and experience of love." And you say, "Great, Mom! I'm on my way." And so you come to do that.

Time, in what is called "earlier times" has been fairly solidified. Now, with the Mother's experience and introduction of Her New Time, those brackets of eternal and infinite are becoming somewhat perforated. Your sense of being anchored fully in linear time is shifting.

Think of it this way, time previously was a frozen pond that you could skate, play and have fun on to your heart's delight, but it was pretty solid. Then, to get ready for the Mother's New Time, there was the Tsunami of Love; now time is more like a beautiful ocean and you are a dolphin, a whale, a school of fish swimming and exploring.

You are not losing your physical body—if anything, you are expanding your awareness and your experience of physicality. You are coming to understand that the physical is a gift, not a burden. You are able to move more freely in and out of what you think of as the currents of time; that is why many of you have been having experiences of alternate past or future lifetimes.

The other thing that is occurring with this slight perforation of the brackets of infinity and eternity is that a sense of unity, love and ecstatic experience is coming through into your space. That is a gift beyond measure!

You are being penetrated by the infinite and eternal. Some of you are and will experience this penetration as joy, bliss, ecstasy and unconditional love. The ability to be within those brackets, experiencing what you came for, is still going on. However, simultaneously, the expansion of what your experience in form is and can be, is much greater than ever before.

This expansion reflects the pattern of the universe. It is taking place because humanity, the collective and each of you, my beloved family, are at a point where you are ready to experience more. You are ready not only to know the joy, but to be the joy. To not only know love but to be the love. That is what this ascension and the anchoring of Nova Earth is all about. It is not about departure. It is not about going anywhere. It is not about abandoning your beautiful, magnificent bodies. It is about being in form upon a physical planet, and knowing the magnificence of who you are and who every other person, plant, and animal on the planet is. The knowing sits in your heart. But my request to thee is that you welcome it into your hip, your toe, your hair and every particle of your being.

Humanity has come a very long way in a very short time. I'm not talking two thousand years; I'm talking in the past several years. You have made greater advancements in the past several years than in one-thousand years. That is something to be proud of and to take heart from.

Part of the acknowledgement and embrace of the deep knowing that you are love and divinity itself means that all the clutter, distraction, false beliefs and drama has to be cleared out and destroyed. Sometimes that feels like a breath of fresh air; other times, it feels as if you have been living in a hovel. You enter your sacred space and it is so filled with garbage and junk, you think, "Oh my gosh, I can't do this."

You don't have to do this clean-up alone. You have infinite help. This is the thing about those brackets to which I refer. The infinite, eternal help is completely available to you. You are not alone. You have never been alone.

The destruction can feel as if you are caught in a violent storm, or as if the ice is cracking beneath your feet. You think you're going to go under the ice and drown. But let me be clear—you're not. So simply go quiet and ask for help.

Be the dolphin, be the whale, be the koi, be the shark. Go and play in the Mother's ocean of New Time and see what you discover. Be fearless. Let the excitement of the currents bring you to where you wish to be. Know, my beloved ones, you don't swim alone; I'm there with you.

Call To Action

Thank you for joining me in this time

when the unity of family; when support and nurturance, defense, encouragement and tolerance is needed. Yes, of course, it has always been needed, but now more so than ever.

So often when I speak to you, I ask you to gird yourselves, to prepare and go forward and practice what I have shared with you, the insights that I have given you. I have asked you to practice miracles. I have told you many times that you are miracle workers. You will do far more than I have ever done, and yet you hesitate, you step back and do not really believe me. Not in your core, not in your guts. I had the same problem with the apostles at times.

I have asked you to embrace joy and to live with that flame in your heart. Now I ask you, my beloved friends, to move into action. The hiatus is over. You ask "What type of action?" It is the action of faith, the action of trust, and the action of purpose. It will no longer do to sit on the sidelines and only be the observer. Oh, I expect you to remain the observer while you are in the thick and furious world. And, I ask you to also be the participant as you spread the love.

Each of you has glanced at your sacred contracts, and there is not one of you whose contract does not include the transmission of love. It does not matter whether you are a healer or teacher or channel or manager of time, space, the anchoring of serenity or the bringing of new thought. It is done in love.

Sometimes I get tired of listening to myself, because my message never changes. It cannot and will not, for it is the message that I am imbued with. It is the core of my being and the core of my heart. I have been birthed from the heart of love, as have you. I am the transmitter of love. I have done that as I have walked the earth thousands of years ago, and I do it today. And I will do it tomorrow. I walk with you again when Archangel Michael's peace is firmly anchored upon this planet. Then you will turn to me and say, "Sure Yeshua, you show up after all the hard work is done." And I will say, "that is only fair—I did it last time."

None of you came to sit in sorrow, sadness or despair. You know that deep inside you. None of you came to sit in inaction. None of you came to be blasé, to not care about what is transpiring within you, around you, and upon the planet. You do not have that capacity. Because of that, you do not have the capacity to indefinitely stand back and not participate in the ways that are appropriate to you.

When I ask you to step forward in action, to do it purposefully, I am asking you to do it with clear intent, but also in ways that are completely appropriate and not timid. It does not mean standing in a corner with one person and saying, "I know about a healing you could try." It does not mean observing the suffering of others. It is stepping forward, and even when you think that your message, actions and love are not welcome, they are. The message may fall on deaf ears, but the action and the love will not. The love will be transmitted. That kindness, that truth, will enter into the heart and being whether it is an entire crowd or one person.

When I ask you to step forward in action, I am not saying don't play, for that is the best way to involve others. Humans have become far too serious and with the elimination of the false grids, they come to realize that that invention no longer serves them. When you engage in laughter, smiles and friendliness, it works.

When I walked the Earth, when I strolled on the shore of the Sea of Galilee, I always invited everybody to come and join me, to walk with me, to talk with me, to be my friend. That is why so many came. My heart and my arms were wide open. I did not say to some, you cannot come, you are excluded. The message of love is inclusion. The action of love is inclusion. All are welcome.

You have had a mighty infusion of hope into your hearts and into the fabric of your countries, but it does not stop there. Yes, step forward in trust, step forward in faith, but do not stop there. I ask you to take the actions of hope that express in concrete ways the ability to change, to transform and to bring this planet forward. Yes, there are more people on the Earth these days—but doesn't that make it easier to reach a bunch all at once?

I do not mean you should not take time for relaxation, reflection, meditation, and prayer. Sometimes you forget the importance of prayer. It is what sustained me in my darkest hour, it is what fortified me when I knew I would lose my family, my friends, and what I had come to love.

Prayer is especially important when you don't understand, and do not think that it is necessary to always understand. It is not. That is called faith. And I don't speak of prayer just of religions, whether it is the Bhagavad Gita, the Torah, the Bible or the Qur'an. I speak of the prayers of your heart. You do not turn to me often enough. When I call you friend, when I call you brother and sister, when I speak of my love for you, my compassion for you. I'm offering my hand. I am offering my help.

Don't think as you go forward in this action, this next step in your evolution that you will not need a helping hand—and not only from me, but from each other, from the circle that supports you. That is why it is important for you to understand the nature of the contract of the Universal Law that governs contracts. It is a coming together in agreement and that agreement is support. That agreement is to support each and every one of you that you may be that transmitter of love. It doesn't matter whether you are shampooing someone's hair or running a corporation. There is blessed equality in the differentiation, in the uniqueness and in the unity.

Nova Earth does not exist without unity and community, and that unity begins within you. You may think that you have been building the foundations of hope and joy and creation, but you haven't. You have built the whole house and you're ready to go.

I am asking you to commit to me with your heart, right now, the actions that you will take to reinforce hope, to practice trust, and to anchor love. Not only within yourself, not only within your circle, but within the collective of humanity. I ask for your assistance and you are ready. It is a call to arms with no guns, no weapons, although you can keep your sword of Archangel Michael. You are armed with the truth. You have eliminated the illusions, as have I, and you are in the alignment of truth. So go forward my friends, but don't forget, or overlook, or in false pride think that you can do it all yourself. You have backup. You have the backup not only of my sacred self, but of this entire Council of which there are many, many humans.

Now in this call to action I close with another request. Take time for tenderness. Take time to be in the place of being in calmness. Take time for the calm, tenderness for yourself and each other. It is what replenishes you. It is as necessary as food, air and water. It is the retreat - that you may step forward yet again. Go with my love, my blessings and my strength.

Stand With Me

I have the honor to speak to you about peace, about my compassion, and about the joy I give you. Look not to pain and sorrow and suffering. I am not saying to turn your head and ignore it, but do not engage; do not add your energy to the pain, suffering and sorrow.

As you travel to help those who are displaced, bring compassion, bring the strength of fortitude, bring the patience of Job, and the mercy of the Mother and Father. This is what is required. It is not to ever override free will and choices of anyone. It is to awaken the compassion; the understanding that you are all Gaians.

I have known invading forces in my life such as the Romans, who were foreign invaders into my land. Although they conquered, or so they thought, they did not subjugate us. The Judaic traditions and my messages live today, long after ancient Rome.

Aggression, control, bloodlust is not of the fabric and tapestry of the Mother—and is not the truth of what it means to be human.

Has humanity been at war for far too long, thousands of years? The era I speak of is over two thousand years old, and war is still going on. The countries change, the players change, but the bloodlust and the desire for control doesn't change, until now.

The energy of your planet, of the Mother's tsunami of love, of Her gifts of clarity and purity and grace will not be denied. The divine qualities of compassion, fortitude, patience, humility and service cannot be downplayed. This is the time when love is restored to the planet, and to the hearts, minds, wills and beingness of every human. The mastery within, expressed in action in the without, comes to the forefront.

My message has never changed. Love yourself first and foremost, and love your neighbors. You are, as much as I am, the child of the Mother/Father/One. You are here to work miracles—or what has been thought of as miracles, because love was never a miracle. It is simply a natural state of being. The miracles come in the actions of love. They are called miracles not because they are alchemical, but simply because they are unfamiliar.

Change is in the air. People, Gaians, are opening their hearts to one another. You are declaring, not in the privacy of your own home, but publically, that terror, hatred, bloodlust, greed, control issues are not acceptable, and not welcomed on this planet in any dimension, in any reality, in any timeline.

You, as wayshowers, do not override free will, but you do set the tone. You set the patterning of how to proceed. You demonstrate what is laudable and lovable, and what is not. Anchor yourself firmly with me, my beloved friends, in this dimension of love today, tomorrow, the day after, and every day for the rest of your life. Let us declare once again, peace on Earth. Not peace on Earth for some, but peace on Earth for all!

Participate in as many joint and conjoint meditations and prayer groups as you can. You are the wayshowers. You are the agents and the angels of change.

I am your servant, your brother, and I am counting on you as I always have, to stand with me and by me. Let us proceed together and let us walk in peace, joy and laughter.

The True Meaning of Service

There is a misconception that masters do not incarnate. Many of us have done so time and again, usually for reasons of service.

Service has a serious connotation on Earth and has come to mean dour, heavy, forgetting how to play, with feelings of self-importance. When I speak to you this day of service, I speak to you of the sheer joy of being alive.

There are times in this existence when each of you has felt, "I am here to be of service and I will trudge on. Father/Mother, I will do your bidding and I will do your service." You think it is a burden you carry on your shoulders. Then you point to me and say, "Look at him. He came and did his service and he had to carry a cross and die. They persecuted him and he didn't even get paid."

When my Mother asked me, "Will you go to Earth and help people remember?" I said, "Sure, I will go. I will embrace the life of a man. I will not forget who I am for that is mastery; it is simply remembering."

By remembering, I do not mean to remember the transcript of each and every life; I mean the deep heart remembering of the essence of who you are. That is truly the service that you bring to Earth; it is the remembering. It is embracing your spirit in form and living your life fully. That is your service.

Each one of you has chosen how you will express this service, how you will express this joy of being in form as teacher, healer, channel, wife, husband, mother, father or friend. But when I talked you into coming, I did not say, "Let us go suffer and die in misery." I said to you, "Let us go play."

There is a density upon this planet that has grown and taken on a life of its own. This density is a human creation. You did not come to suffer. You came to be and hold the light of God in physical form. You came to be the voice, mind, will, actions and life of who you are.

Your service is breathing. Your service is waking up in the morning and being glad of being alive and of who you are. It is being absolutely in the moment.

There is another component to service, which is being entwined with others. Entwined is service. It means embracing, putting your hands into another's. That is why you do two fingers to the heart. You are not simply touching a person's chest; you are entwining their heart, weaving and joining with them. That is service. We could replace the term service with play and you would get more clearly the idea of what I am speaking about. It is not drudgery; it is not work. It is what brings sheer joy to you.

Have there been creations of hardship, darkness and density? Yes. And that is when you turn to each other and say, "Let us go together and diffuse this through laughter and joy."

Are there moments of heartbreak? Yes. You are human. You are masters in the making, and in that role you will find your ability, not to ignore the pain and suffering on your planet—for that is why you have compassion, hope, and the gift of fortitude—but to break through all of that and get to the smile.

You are the "heart and smile" repair person. That is what you do. It does not matter how you go about it other than extending yourself to others. You did not choose to go into the void; you chose to come to planet Earth to restore love. That is the Plan and your purpose. It is an exact mirror of who you are. If you were not of joy you would not care or be affected by the pain and suffering of others. Their pain would not touch your heart. But you came to live in community and to interact with others.

In each one of you there still lurks a feeling of despair at times. Many of you have turned to me and asked, "What's the point? What was the point of your life, Jesus, and what is all this work for if it is only to end in defeat and suffering, pain and loss?"

The point is to keep going. You are the ones who will go forward and share the love with your friends, families and neighbors.

It is a shame so many of my stories of laughter, love and fellowship have been lost. Those messages of hope are what my friends and disciples went forward to share with everyone. Not just hope of redemption, for who really cares about the next life when you are sitting at the table with food to eat and share? It was hope of love, of being embraced, of embracing the sweetness of your own divinity shining through.

Many of you have been fearful about having your light shine through. You have been tried, found guilty, tortured, maimed, and murdered for these beliefs, and for that shining through. But that fear is only based in memory. It is still your purpose to allow yourself to shine through, and you do not do that in solitary confinement. You do not do that sitting by yourself. You do it by sharing this hope and joy of who you really are—with another, and then another and another.

Each of you has had the experience of meeting your true love, of someone you cherished, and saying to somebody else, "You won't believe I met somebody and they are so wonderful. They are filled with light and they make me laugh. My heart is expanding and I feel whole when I am with them."

Think of having that feeling, that knowing, about yourself each and every moment of every day. It is not boastful, for you do not need to speak of it in that way; but that energy, that brightness will shine through.

When you turn to me and ask, "Jesus, what should I do? What is my service? How am I to go about my role in the fulfillment of the Mother's plan?" I reply, "Go play." That is why so many of you are being freed up—and why after you have been freed up. Many of you are realizing that what you really love to play at is your sacred work. Do what brings you joy. In that, you do your service.

There will be times when you will feel like you have been hit with a four by four and you will turn to me and say, "Jesus, this does not feel like joy. This feels like crucifixion; it feels like pain, anguish, suffering, grief and loss." It would be foolish and dishonest for me to deny this, for that is also part of the journey of destroying human illusion.

There are moments of devastation and there are moments when you say, "I don't know if I can go on. I don't know if I wish to do this anymore." When that happens, go within your heart and feel my presence with you.

Know that within my heart, within your heart, there still lies love and joy. You do not need to do anything other than simply breathe. Allow this feeling of despair to pass from you until you can grow with the joy again and embrace it.

Do not make denials of what is very obvious and in front of your face. Understand it; it will teach you compassion. It will teach you fortitude, even while you feel that you have had enough of those lessons.

When you do not know what to do, stay still. Stay still and go to the spark where I am within you, and simply be. When you cry, know that you cry the tears of millions. When you laugh, know that you laugh the laugh of God. It will reverberate throughout the universe. When you are feeling whole again, turn outward and re-engage in your community, with your circle and your loved ones.

This is not about living a life free of grief, sorrow, pain and suffering; they are the illusion you are breaking through and clearing for the restoration of love. But to deny them prolongs them.

When you are ready again, go out and play. If it is not play and is not giving you joy, then do not do it. It is that simple. If you are eating poison and it is making you sick, then stop. Play in community, in interaction with others. You don't unfold alone, you entwine with others.

We will do this together, for there is no

191

greater gift to any universe than to be in the heart of One and to be in form. That is the service you will share with others; the play and the joy you will give to yourself and to all of us.

You are ready. You have been called and you have answered. It is a time of dramatic change; it does not come from Wall Street or the White House or the Kremlin. It comes from you.

Earth's Creator Race

I want to explain a little more about creation and about the term Creator Race. It is not a race of supremacists—quite the contrary. It is a race of humble human beings who are the embodiment of grace and the embodiment of love.

Often, we've talked about the creation of this wonderful planet of Gaia, and how it was created as a planet of love and a planet of peace. We cannot have a planet of war and have love present at the same time. We cannot have a planet where there are the false paradigms of control and greed, anger and lust, and have love present at the same time.

In the very creation and the essence of this mighty being called Gaia, was the formation of a place, a physical experience of such diversity and incredible beauty that the angels would come and play here, to know what it was to have a physical experience of love.

The planet was created in majesty. Nothing went unattended: from dewdrops to oceans, forget-me-nots to the redwood forests, from the grain of sand on the beach to the Rocky Mountains and the Himalayas. Nothing was overlooked; the diversity, the splendor. How could an angel not come here and feel that they were in the heart of magic and still connected to all of us at home? That has always been the function of this place, and the act of service that Gaia performs for the Mother.

When the first beings came, their lineage, as you tend to think of it, was angelic. Part of the joy, the fun of the beings who arrived at the very start (long before your recorded history) was to create. The physical playground had been created. But what the first race, the original Creator Race did was to create experiences, activities, the joys of physicality. Most of that physical experience was not just of having a body but of having emotion, persona and mental facility as well. Now that was an enormous creation! Then they arrived and began to answer the question, "So what will we do with it?" And the creation has never stopped.

Over many thousands of years, the illusions, the false paradigms have gained a foothold very deep in the hearts and the minds of the collective. But still, that kernel of knowing, of being able to create, has never gone away—whether it is creating a child, a family, a business, a flower garden.

So we shake our heads in confusion and disbelief when human beings say, "I cannot create." It is just that the process has been slightly skewed.

It was my choice and my joy to come to Earth. I do not want to hear about the martyr, that is absurd. Did I have moments of sadness? Of course. So do you. But let me tell you, it was my choice to come. It was my profound joy to have my feet in the desert sand and in the water; to hold a newborn, to witness the flowers in the spring, to gaze at someone I loved.

My purpose, and our plan, was that if I could resurrect and re-instill that fundamental understanding, that operational belief system of love once again, then beings would get back on track. Because that operational belief system of love is what was lost in the darkness; that is what had been lost in the Creator Race.

The illusion of separation and isolation had grown. So I came to remind everybody of love: that love would resurrect anything, that it would conquer anything—even death, blindness, poverty or hunger.

On Earth there are great debates whether I succeeded or not. But let me assure you, on our side there is no doubt," That's because more than two-thousand-years later you are still talking about me.

I do not care if any deny me—it is the love I don't want them to deny. What is happening now in your time, in your place,

is this resurgence of love. Love is the answer. It is the answer to all the breakdowns of the systems you are witnessing, the systems that have been built on false beliefs, which you would call shifting sand. It is good news!

The key, the answer, and the core of recreating this experience of being on Earth is love. It is letting go of all the illusions and stepping into the knowing that you are a creator; that your best friend is a creator, that Gaia is a creator, and that we are co-creators with you.

You cannot continue to say of the detractors, "Oh, it is the forces of darkness and evil and they are having a battle." We are well aware of that. Realize, it is not an even battle, because where love shines all illusions evaporate.

I want you to love the oil in your Gulf of Mexico, uranium in the Sea of Japan, debris in the middle of the Pacific Ocean. I want you to love it so much that it evaporates. That is your next assignment in concert with Gaia. This acknowledgement that you are the creators is what has shifted.

You ask, "Well, why are we now the Creator Race?" The reason is, you woke up! You have anchored your divinity! Time to get busy! We will help you. We will serve you. We will coach you. We will do your tasks and we will do your bidding.

Acknowledge and cherish who you are. This is the greatest gift of the Mother and Father. In reality, the gift of love is the only gift. It may take many forms, but the energy of the universe is love. Like me, resurrect and remember. Help others remember: Love is the key. It is the key to Heaven, but it is also the key to Earth.

Step Forward in Truth

Often, I refer back to my life in Galilee, Bethlehem, and Palestine because it was a life filled with joy, not defeat.

It was not only my sacred wife who knew of my impending death, but my sacred circle as well. They did not know the time or the hour or the unfoldment of how, but I prepared them long beforehand. We spoke as well, of what would happen after I was gone. The teachings were to be shared freely with all who came with any interest.

Many of them said, "Lord, I don't know how to teach, or how to heal like you. I do not know how to conduct a ceremony, or see into the hearts of others like Magdalena. I do not know if I will be able to continue without you at my side."

I would always laugh, and in the laughter we would dispel the worry. We would talk as brothers and sisters and comrades about what the true fear was. It always came to this: "If I step forward and teach, that means that you, dear Jesus, will not be with me and my heart will break. I will feel abandoned and lonely and I will not know how to proceed."

This is the time of the unfoldment we have waited for, and we thought would happen thousands of years ago. We didn't understand the Greeks and Romans were not ready, to say nothing of the Assyrians, but we never stopped trying. Many of the stories have become convoluted, but that is the way of oral history and legend. The truth has never changed, and it is true in all religions, all belief systems.

Even those who claim themselves as atheists love their neighbors as themselves in order to keep good civil order. You treat the other person as you desire to be treated; with compassion, understanding, courtesy and honoring. You do this not only to them, but their family, their lineage and from whence they came.

This is something in your society that is being lost; it is the sense of who you are, of your people, of your soul family and your biological family. For even when your family has been horrendous, they have gifted you and they have anchored within you that deep knowing of who you are.

I am asking you to step forward, and if you do it, I'll do it, too. The good news is I have your back. Don't worry, you are surrounded by the Mighty Ones, the archangels and by this sacred Trinity that holds you so dear.

Don't think the teaching simply takes place in the classroom, that is not so. It takes place in the shops, the classrooms of universities, the clinics and the counseling sessions. It takes place in so many forms. That teaching is the acknowledgement of the divinity of the human spirit that stands in front of you.

How can you possibly gaze in awe at the Grand Canyon, the ocean, the eagle, the Alps, the dolphins, and not be in awe when you stare at a fellow human being? The ability to judge and dismiss is the cancer of the human race. It creates and reinforces that other cancer of lack of self-worth, from the smallest child to the ones who are elderly and sit alone in their chairs because "they are not worth the time."

Such attitudes are not of love. Look at who stands in front of you. Rediscover the sense of awe of humanity—for that is the quality of Nova Being. Truly see what is transpiring and hold it up so that others will see it as well.

Every human being has come to Earth in grace. The terrible misunderstanding of original sin has been perpetuated and then built upon, but I tell you: There is not one being that did not come with grace as part of their design, and in the core of their heart the essence of grace is still there.

It is up to you to expand that, to allow it to come forward, to remind the person of this truth. Remind them that they too are a child of God.

This is the truth of the universe. Let us tell everyone! Step forward and be the speakers of truth. Be the clarion trumpets

of true abundance. Pick up your horn of Archangel Gabrielle and speak. Do not fear; we are with you. Go in peace.

Dream Nova Earth

You are in a time of massive, rapid change. That is the best news I can bring to you, for it is what we have all awaited. While we have had many conversations about the creation and co-creation of Nova Earth and Nova Being, I wish to now speak to your heart intimately about dreaming. I am asking you to take more time to dream, visualize, and allow your heart and mind to soar in the new reality. You are not arriving in the new reality with it all pre-constructed; this is not a prefab situation.

There are many elements in place, and there are elements such as false grids and belief systems, that will absolutely be missing as you leave behind the old paradigms of the old third dimension. That is good news to all of us and certainly to all of you.

Out of the dreaming comes what you are choosing to create as well as the unity of your being and this circle. It is what you wish to bring forward in terms of environments and, concretely, in terms of buildings, situations, institutions and ways of doing things.

My beloved wife, my Magdalena, and I used to spend a great deal of time together dreaming. Each of us was fully aware of the very likely unfoldment of our life and our family's life together during my incarnation as Jesus, and hers as Mary Magdalene. But that did not stop us from dreaming.

The reason I bring this up, my dear hearts, is that she and I dreamed this time when peace would be restored, when love would reign on Earth, when freedom would be the air that all beings breathed. This time when sweetness would be the way, and gentleness would be the watchword of how people would treat each other and how communities would live and thrive. The foundation was laid so long ago.

The Divine Plan of our Mother is not only infinite; it is eternal. But this portion of it, this fulfillment of it, and this vision of it was something that Mary and I spent much time thinking, dreaming and talking about, because it made it all worthwhile. We know that in human terms, time sometimes stretches and you say, "When will this take place? When will we see the tangible shift?"

My beloved friends, you are the tangible shift. Look in the mirror and see how you perceive yourself and your world around you. You are moving fully into your role as Creator Race, and that is why I am asking you to join my beloved and I in the dreaming. Frankly, my friends, most of you are dreaming too small.

I do not in any way wish to minimize your burdens: for some of you it is health challenges, for some it is money and finance, for some it is the loneliness as you yearn for your spiritual family and your unique partner. I do not minimize this, because I know of the heaviness of your heart.

I do ask you to just set that slightly aside, as if you were constructing something out of building blocks or Legos on a dining room table. Take those worries and put them off in a corner to your right-hand side where we can take care of them.

Then leave the rest of the table clear for your dreaming and building. In that construction of the reality, all of those old issues which are simply telltale signs of the old third dimension will be addressed.

As you are dreaming, dream of community, so you are not simply etherically holding hands with those you love, but that you are gathered around that dining room table. You are holding hands as you give blessings for the food that you have all co-created. You are sharing laughter and sweetness. Hold that vision and that closeness so that it is repeated up and down the streets of every community all over your planet. Hold that vision so that there is food on every table, fresh water to drink, and if it is a wedding, I will provide the wine.

I am asking you to expand your vision and begin to truly build, because it is all underway. It is not some distant date; you are already shifted. Gaia is firmly entrenched in the fifth through the seventh dimensions. Your feet are upon her; therefore, it is only the idea and the belief system of the old third dimension that remains.

Yes, the Mighty Ones, the Archangels Michael, Raphael, Uriel, Jophiel and our beloved Gabrielle are very busy cleaning up that old third dimension. So don't concern yourself with it. I want you to go for this dream of a new tomorrow with the ease, grace and crystal clear clarity that you already have.

If you are not clear, if you are not sure, then come to the 13th Octave and rest there. Come to the Warehouse of Heaven and collect the codes and create. We are willing to help you because we are your family as clearly as you are each other's family. We love you and there is nothing we would not do to assist you as you are assisting us, as each of you is fulfilling my Mary's and my dream.

Let us go forward together in this creation and co-creation. Let there be no such thing as even a hint of a breeze that says "limitation." Dream your world, because it is Terra Nova; it is yours and it is mine. Then we can return and walk together, and this I look forward to. Go with my love and go in peace my sweet family.

Homage to Earth

I invite you to pay homage to this glorious planet you walk upon that nurtures you as both mother and father, and to also pay homage to yourself. You have chosen to be a creature of Earth, spirit in form—to walk this planet in union with your brothers and sisters of every kingdom and species.

Know that we join you in this celebration of life. It is time, my friends, to fully embrace your physical form—to cherish and nurture it as you have never done before. In so doing, you nurture this planet: this garden of green, this garden of delight.

You have come to this dimension, to this time and place to have the experience of physicality, to join in perfect union with spirit. You cannot do this by divorcing form. So, as you walk upon the Earth, anchor within your bodies: rejoin the form you have chosen, glory in the mind that is your partner and your creation. Laugh and play because this is the planet of fun, of joy, of wholeness—not of pain. It is my planet of love.

As you travel homeward to the heart of One and anchor within you this wholeness, know that I take your hand. Know that as you walk this path, I walk with you.

You have chosen to walk the Earth during this time of miracles. Know this is the miracle of your life as well, and the miracles you are choosing at this moment to create—with us and for us and for thy sacred selves. The mother planet renews herself and enters into her radiance; do so with her.

197

Heal The Wounds

You are the children of my universe, life and heart. This is our reunion on Earth during the time of reawakening of my race, of my brothers and sisters. We come together now to heal the wounds that each of you has inflicted upon yourself and upon each other over eons; to embrace the love that you are and your love for each other.

It is timely to remember, not only the times that you have been wounded, but also when you have been the aggressor. Remember the wounds you inflict upon yourself in grief and guilt are a waste of time and energy, and certainly a waste of a lifetime. I ask you to remember where the fear lurks within thee and eradicate it from your life forever. There is no time and no room in this reality for this to reoccur.

Each of you has walked with me, not only in Galilee but in the healing councils when we have gathered to heal this planet and the universes. We do it again, knowing that this time it will be a victory filled with love and laughter and joy.

I call to you this day to celebrate with devas, fairies and elements, so you can remember the joy of being human and embrace spirit in form, your form, your body. Most of you have spent your lives trying to escape these wonderful vessels. You have chosen to come to this planet to assume form and spread love. I do this with you, not as master, not as teacher, but as friend and companion.

Don't even think of hierarchy, for that is a thing of the past. It is time for this planet to embrace a new understanding of being. Each of you is of the new ray, wayshowers, first in line pathfinders. This does not make you on top; it simply makes you out front. But I will walk with you, as many of us will, for you are loved and cherished beyond measure, beyond time and beyond this universe that you cherish. Turn to us.

Do not look for miracles beyond your fingertips, for those you call saints never sought to be so. They purified, loved and said, "Yes." Sacrifice is a dirty word in your vocabulary. It has come to mean "a placing aside" rather than a "joining to." Sacrifice is a union of soul and purpose. It is an alignment not only with your own needs, pathway, inclination and soul; it is a union with the Will and Unfoldment of One. The unfoldment of this planet is why you are here.

The Mother has birthed this garden of paradise long ago and it has been desecrated. I struck a deal with my Father long ago to return balance to Earth. There is no expiration date on this undertaking, but I tell you my brothers and sisters, before you came, you turned to me and said, "Yeshua we will join you again and we will succeed. We will succeed in laughter, joy and renewal, for you cannot recreate paradise and restore the Mother's plan with tears and agony, war and defeat."

Yes, I walk in the dangerous places. I negotiate the treaties and remind many of who is truly in charge. I do not do this gently. I do it clearly and firmly, but I never coerce. The freedom of mankind, of all races is too dear to my heart. But, when one is blinded by Light, vision immediately clears. When we gather as One, unified in heart, this small speck in a multitude of universes will shift the axis of power throughout. It is Universal Law and what you think of as chain reaction. Let us proceed together this day and always as One.

Gifts from the Void

I come to speak about being in the void, in the stillpoint; the state I resided within while in the tomb. It is being in the All and the nothingness—where the new is created, formulated, and brought forth.

Many of you have difficulty with going and holding the stillpoint, even for the recommended seventeen seconds. It is not a long time, is it? Think of spending a long period, thirty three hours, in stillpoint. Think of the magnificent things I have created during that hiatus of in-between.

Often, when you are in this place of stillpoint, you do not go deep enough. Or, if you are in the void, you think nothing is happening and feel you must jump out and get busy, move into action. But this is not so. This is your ego speaking to you; the one that is afraid you will die. If nothing else,

the example of my life long ago has taught you that no one dies, no one disappears, and existence is infinite, expanding and eternal.

There is no rush to leave the stillpoint or the void. You will not only survive, you will thrive. By having gone to the void, that place of darkness and light, you will resurrect yourself, in a very different way. For it is not my resurrection I want to talk about, but yours.

Let me be very clear, there is a difference between stillpoint, the void, and being stuck. Many of you have felt you are stuck because things aren't moving the way you expect or anticipate, when in fact you are simply in the void. Within the void is the stillpoint; you cannot get to the stillpoint without entering through and into the void. It is like walking into a completely dark room, sitting down in the middle of it, and finding that center of absolute peace and nothingness.

Do not hurry to leave there. Do not judge what you think of me and my place of resting—my tomb—for those thirty-three hours. Do not worry, because just as my beloved wife Mary came to arouse me, as we had prearranged and as I had promised, someone will come and arouse you.

If it is not a human, it will be me. You will feel my love sweep over you and awaken you, and call you forward back out of the stillpoint into the light of action, because it is a time of action that is upon us. Now, my friends, is a time of stepping forward and declaring yourself, not in egotistical ways, not in ways that are abrasive, but in ways that are kind, considerate, gentle and loving. Ways which are reflective of the truth of who you are.

When you are in the void, you are learning to be multidimensional. Sometimes this puts you off-kilter, and it even puts your body off-kilter. Again, do not judge it. Tend to your body, tend to that sense of imbalance and keep going because, my beloved friends, you are needed.

You are the messengers for Earth. If you do not speak, who does? If you do not teach and heal, who does? You know the agreement with my Mother: I am not to return to Earth in physical form until peace reigns.

The tipping point is here, my friends. We are ready. Are you? Call upon us; call upon me. I will show you the brilliance of your own resurrection, of the embodiment of your own divinity. I will gladly be your mirror, as you are mine. You are not alone in this and neither are we. Nothing changes and yet it is all changed. You are the forefront. You are the changers of the world.

There is a sense, or an opinion sometimes that Mother/Father/Me/Holy Spirit will create infinitely and forever—that this is what we do. But the pivotal part of this creation of Nova Earth and Nova Being is the co-creation with you, the human beings.

You have evolved from the hunter-gath-erer to the manufacturer, to the information gatherer, and now to Creator Race. You have progressed full circle and you stand with us, angelic in form, with full ability to create. If we keep doing it for you, rather than with you, you will not remember this key factor.

Part of our soul agreement with you is that you will remember this key factor and ability and bring it forth, thereby transforming and eliminating old paradigms of lack, need and limitation. The torture of children, adults, animals, plants and trees will be history; human beings will love each other as they love themselves, and will reach out to their neighbor with an open hand— not a clenched fist.

This is what you are doing with us. The sacred nature of our mission together cannot be minimized or underestimated.

Come and join me today; travel back with me. Take the time and spend it with me in the tomb, in the void, in the still-point, that we may rise together in victory.

Peace Now

Peace is the promise of the Mother; it is Her ultimate promise to you. It is also the chore and task of many above and below. But the message is the same; for when we tell you not to embrace the chaos, to stay within your sacred being of calm serenity and love, to stay within your shield, to stay within the eye of your hurricane, that is what is required—practically and literally—to create peace upon this planet.

Physical action of human beings is required to create peace on Earth right now. When there is hysteria, a shadow of fear or doubt about your own efficacy and power, there is no peace. Bad men will not be allowed to destroy this planet. There are many who wish to return home to the light and to the love, and they will be permitted to do so, but they are not permitted to take all with them, including Mother Earth.

Let us be very clear on that. There will not be nuclear devastation and there will not be an all-out war; but peace is very different. It comes from the heart of each one of you, united as one, as one force stronger than the gale wind that now blows. You are doing this, and you are doing magnificently. Do not pay attention to those who would scare you and defeat you, for your strength is within you and between you. You have this power and you are the physical vessels of creation—not next year, not last year, but right now in your reality.

You have been given the gift of moving beyond what you have known as the time and space continuum. That means, dear friend, that you are free to bi-locate wherever you choose. Go and walk the streets of Iraq, Iran or Syria and bring messages of peace—each and every night, each and every day. Triple yourself; send yourself to the plains of Africa and feed the starving children that they will know peace. Go to your inner cities in your own country and clothe and shelter the homeless that they will know peace. Peace is very different than the simple absence of war machines. It is the promise of the Mother, and you are doing this work on Her behalf. She is very proud of you.

The power is within you. I walk with you—not as an unseen force, but as brother of your heart. Go in peace.

Embrace The Change

Welcome my beloved ones, welcome to this time of new time, change of reality, unification of heart, and glorious acceptance of who you are. Yes, this is a time of fulfillment, of change, of unity and community and of letting go.

Each of you have had experiences where a loved one or a child is crying and fighting you and trying to get away; then comes the moment of release when the loved one or the child simply melts into your arms and into your heart and allows the love to flow. That is what I want you to do with us—with the Mother, the Father and I, your guides and the Council of Love. It is also what I ask you to do with your sacred self and each other, for this is unity. You cannot have separate pieces of who you are, and you cannot have separate pieces of your family of soul and your family of humanity.

Yes, it is a time of change, and I know that many of you seek the physical symbols of change—and you will have it in spades. But it will also manifest within you: in your life and what you are choosing to co-create, not only with us but also with Gaia.

Beloved ones, Gaia has shifted, whether you know it, acknowledge it, embrace it or not; and you have shifted. Is it subtle? Yes. Is it dramatic? Yes. A significant piece of this is letting go of what you have previously thought of as drama; there is no need or place for it.

In previous times, you have used drama as a catalyst—not only to change, but also to learn, expand and reach a place of knowing. Now you have passed that point. You reclaim yourself as creator and co-creator, and I welcome you.

Long ago, when I would walk and talk with family, friends, acquaintances, allies and in some cases even enemies, they would say to me, "Jesus, these changes that you seek—of loving yourself and loving your neighbor—are beautiful and I agree with you, or I disagree with you. But I do not think that it is realistic to think that everything is going to change, that society is going to embrace what you say." And I would look them right in the eye and touch their heart and say, "It depends on you."

Some agreed, some remained skeptical, some turned away. It did not matter because the message did not change. It was carried forward and it grew until humanity reached this point, individually and collectively, where all you want is love, peace and joy. There are many add-ons, many frills, but that is the core of it. This desire is not something you are slowly arriving at; it is already present. The yearning, the insistence, the commanding and demanding is already there as you seek unity with one another, with yourself, with Gaia, and with us who will walk the planet yet again.

There will be tangible change. But understand you are co-creating this with us. It is not being done to you or for you; it is being done with you, because you are capable of it. You always have been. I am not skeptical; I am overjoyed that the fulfillment of the promise is finally underway.

My beloved friends, my brothers and sisters, this is victory. And it is ours. Embrace the change; it is what you have waited for, what we all have waited for, and it is now.

The Gifts of Nova Earth

Laughter is the key to your heart. It increases your vibration, and is the expression of joy. In this, I mean genuine laughter, not at the expense of another and never in cruelty. It is the laughter of knowing that you are truly united with all. It is the sense of glee, be it buttercup or butterfly, that you are all one.

Earth has ascended to her magnificent self, and you have done so with her. It is time that many will join you. We share with you the tools of the trade, but primarily welcome you home, to my home, yes, to the heart of One; to the seventh dimension where we will bring and keep you from now on. Yes, you have free choice, obviously to return to the third dimension, but none of you have lived there for sometime, so it would be a strange recurrence. Know this; it is the seventh dimension of love and joy where we reside. It is where I have always lived and will walk again with you on the green fields of Earth.

We will walk by the cleansed waters and we will gaze at the pristine stars and we will welcome our friends from far and near. We will talk to the dolphins, the whales, the dogs, the cats and the snakes. We will talk finally to each other, clearly without hesitation, from heart to heart. Each of you knows that the seventh dimension of Christ consciousness is where you have lived and where you anchor when you speak from your heart. Now you are teaching others to have similar conversation in the physical reality of the seventh. We intend to accomplish this in laughter, tears of laughter, joy and outrageous humor. Please come with me. Walk with me.

Through the Portal to the Cities of Light

Often, people have thought that going through the portal means death and dying;

the removal of the physical form. That is not what it means at all, for even when I died up on the cross, what did I do but grab the sidebars and jump through the portal? You saw me later in my radiant light form, free to do as I wished and to serve in ways that have changed the world.

I don't ask that you abandon your physical form, quite the contrary. I ask you to jump into your bodies as you have never done before. Go through that portal through your heart, and embrace your physical being.

Many of you are experiencing aches and pains, and exhaustion because your body is adjusting to hold this vibration of light, of Nova Being. Although you complain bitterly, you have said, "Yes." Go with the flow and allow your body to adjust. Welcome these changes.

There also is another meaning for going through the portal. When you go through the portal of physicality, you are also opening that corridor between your cities and the future cities of light. You want to walk in these cities of light to meet your brothers and sisters of crystalline beauty, to join with them and the many races that inhabit these cities.

Go through the portal. When you come back to this reality, you are bringing that energy and anchoring it into your physicality. You are anchoring the cities of light.

I assure you after waiting eons; you don't

want to miss it. I bring you messages of joy, laughter, and gladness. Many of you have felt disheartened and ask, "We have tried this so many times, Lord. When will it work? Is this truly the time, or am I being foolish?" I understand, because I have found myself hung up against the wall, abandoned and destroyed. This is not that lifetime. This is the resurrection of humanity; this is the resurrection of Nova Earth, Nova Being, and Nova You.

I have said to you for years, "I will walk with you on Earth." Where did you think we would be? It is in the new reality; it is in the new place of love.

I am calling to you. Clear your hearts and clear your bodies. Let go of the debris and come walk with me. I am waiting.

AFTERWORD

Greetings, I am Jesus Sananda. I am Yeshua, I am Yeshi. I am Jesus. You know me by many names and you know me as brother, friend, ally, and champion. Not a champion for myself, rather, a champion of you. I've beckoned you and asked each and every one of you to walk with me, but now I expand upon this. I ask you to talk with me, to experience with me, to express with me, and to put into action love.

This is my call to action. It is Archangel Michael's call to action; it is Archangel Gabrielle's call to action; it is Sanat Kumara's call to action, and we do so on behalf of our Mother, the Father and, the One.

Now is the time of unfoldment of the Mother's Plan, of the fulfillment of Her dreams, Her desires, Her Plan. And what is that my beloved friends? It is the re-anchoring and rebirth of love upon this planet, our beloved Earth. What does this look like? What does Nova Earth look like? What does a Nova Being look, feel, sound, and taste like? It certainly isn't complacency.

Love is not merely a feeling, it is the essence and expression of divinity. It is the expression of the Mother/Father/One. It is the experience of the Mother/Father/One. Think of what I say–our Mother, the Divine Mother is constant and ever-changing.

And in the conjunction, the conjoining of the Mother/Father/One is the infinite and eternal action of creation. It does not stop and start, it does not halt or interrupt, it is infinite and eternal, expansiveness, wondrous and phenomenal. And so are you. You also are infinite and eternal. You are patterned by and from the Mother. You are of the Mother, and that means you are of the Father.

Therefore, you are also a being of infinite, eternal creation on a very practical level. You know this and you have experienced this by the construct of aging. You are not the same person who was at the beginning of this conversation, for you have taken many breaths since that time. You have had random thoughts and many emotions. You have created a continuum of life and existence, simply by being who you are. You create subtly and some of you, not so subtly, by intending to continue on living and breathing, being and expanding.

There are many I could speak to about expansion and they would not have the foggiest notion what I was talking about. You do. As love-holders, as lightworkers, I call

you to step forward in the fulfillment of the Mother's Plan.

Make and implement the decision to be the fulfillment of the Plan. In every breath be the expression of your divine design, of your mission and purpose. We not only beckon you, we stand next to you, we walk with you, we run with you, we breathe with you. You, not some stranger, but each of you are the implementers of the Mother's Plan.

It is not through intention only, it is through action. You have been given the insight, the understanding, the tools, the mechanisms, and the will to bring forth your plan within the Mother's Plan and they are in alignment. Your heart and mind are in the alignment of love.

And so I beckon you to your new life, from the moment you awaken. And even in your dream time, you are extraordinarily busy.

But my question to you is, as we walk together is that commitment, are those actions, thoughts and feelings in alignment not only with our Mother but with you? Are they a reflection and the implementation of who you are?"

As I have walked as man, as father and husband, I know what it is to have an off day. I know what it is to be in a bad mood. I also know when you push that aside, surrender it, look at it and laugh and say "oh my goodness, there I go again" and return to the joy and love what is there. More joy and love. So, why would any other choice, any other state of being, any other expression of will make any sense?

You are in your heart consciousness. You have already decided and chose unity and community. What I am asking of you my beloved friends and family, is with me, with Archangels Michael and Gabrielle, with Sanat Kumara, with all of us in the name of the Mother/Father/One, will you take the next step with me?

APPENDIX
THE 13TH OCTAVE

The 13th Octave is a process of Divine Union, one which involves preparation and clearing; initiation, meditation and sacred ceremony; anchoring and consistency. This gift was not available on Earth prior to 1995 when it was bestowed from the heart of One upon humanity as a gift of Divine Kindness.

The realm of human existence on this planet is restricted or defined by the realm of twelve planes, twelve cycles of existence, twelve dimensions. That's the framework for this planet. Before the opening of the 13th Octave, one had to die, to transition, in order to achieve this level of Divine Union. This state of being could not be anchored in a human body and psyche, it was too large. But through this gift of the 13th Octave, the process became available for humanity to break out of the paradigm of Old Earth and re-anchor in the state of Oneness that was the original intent of the Divine Mother for her beloved angels in form.

This shift is so fundamental that many people can't grasp it. The fact that you can be fully anchored and connected in and to the heart of God, operating in the seventh dimension of the Christ consciousness and manifesting in the third dimension just seems beyond comprehension. But that is exactly where entry and anchoring in the 13th Octave places you.

Archangel Gabrielle puts it this way: "To date, that was all that was truly available to those within your energy grid of twelve planes and twelve existences. This has now changed. God created the next energy plane, the next circle long ago, but it has never been open or available to those in physical form on Earth. That is why it initially will be difficult for some to understand and accept. Those in a state of advanced knowing, those who through their daily ritual of joining with the Divine will be the least resistive. They have always known that there was much more beyond the veil, they have always prayed that they would enter the next phase alive, conscious and ready."

The true impact of the 13th Octave is experiential rather than mental or logical. It is beyond the explanations given by traditional religions of relationship with God. And yet ultimately even as words fail us, we need to find rational ways in which to explain this awesome gift to our fellow human beings. We need to find ways in which to reach out, penetrate the chaos, and explain how there is another route to finding wholeness. And the route is painless, supported above and below, achievable, and ecstatic in nature. Initiation and anchoring within the 13th absolutely changes everything—old struggles die away and become dim memories.

Most of us have had moments when we have felt absolutely loved and at peace, when we have experienced the rightness of the Universe. Sometimes, it is simply a momentary flash, experienced when the heart is open, oft times by the majesty of nature or the birth of a child. The other universal experience for most of humanity is the unnamed yearning, the depth of unanswered longing that sits within us and that we do not know how to resolve. It is not eliminated by a sense of belonging and love of partner or family; it does not disappear with success, time or fortune, good or bad. This longing, this sense of a fundamental connection that has been unplugged and needs to be repaired is part of the very make-up of humanity. What we offer, as bringers of the 13th Octave process, is a way to repair that faulty connection, a way in which to re-establish unity and balance, a way to not only momentarily experience love but to expand it in such a way that each person is the Love.

Archangel Gabrielle tells us that all we ever need to get home, to complete our journey to wholeness is love, trust, forgiveness, unity, connectedness and balance. She has said, "the keys to heaven are trust and forgiveness, the pathway is unity, connectedness and balance, the doorway is Love."

This seems so simple and clear. And yet ultimately achieving and maintaining these qualities, this embedded formula, is a life-long challenge. I have seen over the years how at different times different aspects of this formula are emphasized by the other side at different points in our evolution. I have also come to realize that this simple phrase contains the meaning of human existence. It also shows us the way out of the cycle of 12:12.

Archangel Gabrielle said to us from the very beginning "the doorway to the 13th Octave beckons you. This gift, this bond melded between above and below, allows all those who seek to know and be the Love, who seek to live wholly and completely in the Christ consciousness of the seventh dimension, to enter. It is our dearest wish that you will do so. Yes, my dear ones, understand that the transition to being present in the seventh dimension is via the 13th Octave." I understand now that this doorway has been open and available in other realms of consciousness for eternity. It was simply not visible to us on Earth. But now it is. The trick isn't keeping the doorway open; it's keeping our collective consciousness open to that possibility.

The Council cautions us up front that the biggest hurdle we will face is the false belief system of self-worth. "Each of you has come to Earth with sacred mission and undertakings. All missions, all purpose is to become and know Love, to place self

beyond choice into perfect alignment with the Heart of One, the Heart of All. Each of you has unique and beautiful ways in which you endeavor to accomplish this task, yet it is always done through the elimination of all lack, the release of all feelings of lack of self-worth. The question of your worthiness does not exist within the mind of One, for this is a given unalterable fact of existence. It is only through human conditioning that you have forgotten that you are one with Love, Source, and Divine Radiance. The 13th Octave is your key to remembering, your invitation to return home to your perfect state of full awareness, knowing and Love. It is where you and all beings belong."

The Council of Love have given us the process to overcome the variety of issues, debris and obstacles that masquerade and distract us from understanding that core issue of lack of self-worth. They have given us dozens of tools and a storehouse of gifts, all in the supreme hope that we will remember who we really are and say yes. They have outfitted us in many ways we cannot imagine, they have stood by us respectfully and lovingly, all so we will go through that doorway and join with One.

The Council of Love realizes that as human beings we will want some practical explanation of the 13th Octave so they tell us right off the bat "The 13th Octave is beyond time or space. It is off your grid or any grid of physicality. It is beyond dimension. It is simply a state of being. Think of an Octave as a universal system of measurement, in this case the measurement of a spiritual undertaking, from beginning to completion. This spiritual process, this leap of faith is made with the assistance of the Earth, who has anchored herself firmly within the thirteenth. Yet, in our humanness, we continue to ask, "yeah but what is it?"

An octave is a system of measurement that, as we understand it, refers primarily to music, to sound. An octave is "the interval of eight diatonic degrees between two tones by the same name, the higher of which has twice as many vibrations per second as the lower." In practical terms what this tells you is that as you go up an octave you don't simply add eight, you double or square it.

Now think of the realm of human existence, twelve planes, twelve dimensions, twelve cycles of existence. Within each dimension there are twelve potential planes on which one can operate. That is why sometimes you feel that someone is on a different page, seeing or experiencing things differently than you, vibrationally different. Now, peeling the onion, think of each plane as an octave. The experiential potential within each plane is twelve to the twelfth power. Then take that and do the same with the twelve dimensions and the twelve cycles. We are now talking about systems of sound measurement that only NASA is able to comprehend.

The important thing to realize is that the 13th Octave is off those charts. Even if you go to the top of the twelfth plane within the twelfth dimension in your twelfth cycle of existence, you still haven't reached the thirteenth. Prior to now you would hit the proverbial glass ceiling. Now, because of this heart opening above and below, you can make the jump.

Archangel Gabrielle has explained the 13th Octave as a musical reference. "It is the point at which the sound and vibration of God is felt, it is beyond hearing, beyond human ears, but it is clearly felt throughout the Universe."

Consider the 13th Octave in terms of sound and musical theory. Music, octaves, are mathematical formulas first enunciated by Pythagoras. He first perceived that the universal language was numbers, and all energy could be expressed in this manner. For example, light and sound waves can be expressed in quantum physics, in numerical codes. What is perceptible to the human eyes and ears are not the full spectrum of what is out there in the universe. What a dog hears and sees is very different than a human. The Hubble space telescope with its the near-ultraviolet, visible, and near-infrared spectra, is able to detect far more than the human eye. We don't need to understand all of the math behind this to grasp the concept. There is far more out there than we have the physical capacity to perceive.

Most thirteeners have reported being

able, once again, to hear the sound of the Universe, the celestial spheres. It is because through clearing, shutting out the white noise of the ego, and opening to the Universe, that this capacity has returned. It is the high-pitched frequency you often perceive.

Archangel Gabrielle tells us "there is sound beyond the sound of the Universe, beyond the celestial spheres, and it is the sound of One, of Love, of the fuel of the Universe. When you hear the sound of the spheres you are hearing the result of that fuel. Go through the portal, past the sound, go through the heart of One to the silence of the 13th Octave. That is where you will find the sound of Love."

ABOUT THE AUTHOR

Linda Dillon had been the channel for the Council of Love (COL, or the Council) since 1984 after a near-death experience from a car accident opened her heart to her true purpose.

As the vehicle for the Council, Linda channels the vibration of pure Love into the hearts of those who come to her. These people are always recognizable by the dramatic personal changes and transformation they are going through. Channelings are for the transmissions of universal information, as well as to assist people to connect and work with their own personal guides.

Linda channels Jesus Sananda, Mother Mary and Yahweh, as well as the ascended

masters such as St. Germaine, Sanat Kumura, and Maitreya, the Apostles and the Archangels, Gabrielle, Michael, Raphael, Uriel and Jophiel. While the energies and personalities of each being are unique, the vibration of Love, pure and simple remains consistent.

Having had a successful career as a health-care executive, Linda understand the need to make spiritual matters hands-on

217

and practical. She teaches workshops and webinars throughout the year and has a worldwide client base who request individual channelings. She is the CEO of the Council of Love, Inc., and an approved Florida Continuing Education provider in energy healing.

Linda resides on the Treasure Coast of Florida and can be reached through her website, www.counciloflove.com.

Other Titles by Linda Dillon

13th Octave LaHoChi
Now in its seventh printing, this is a how-to book for
the practitioner of the energy healing.

The Great Awakening: A Spiritual Primer
The definitive guidebook leading you through the process of
raising your vibration into the fifth and seventh dimensions.

*The New You: Emerging into the Brilliance of Humanity's
Heart Consciousness*
Discover how you can live each and every day from a place of joy,
hope and grace as you embody love and live in alignment with the
Universal Laws and the Divine Qualities.

These books can be found at the Spirit Store,
www.thespiritestore.net

More Praise for The Jesus Book

The *Jesus Book* spoke powerfully to my heart and soothed my soul.
-Traci Ortega, Media Consultant

As I read *The Jesus Book* I can feel the love of Jesus and my connection to him.
-Robyn Swick, Marketing Executive

The *Jesus Book* enhances our understanding of the messages of Jesus-then and now.
-Lorraine McGovern, Professional Mediator

I melted into these words, remembering, and walking with Sananda again.
-Barbara Olsen, Midwife & Pastoral Student

So easy to read, and hits right in my heart of deep truth.
-Andrea Quagenti, Creative Writer

This opportunity to deeply know Jesus as he actually talks to us is extraordinary!
-Megann Thomas, Owner, Buffalo Spirit
Animal Sanctuary & Energy Medicine Practitioner

61555745R00124

Made in the USA
Charleston, SC
21 September 2016